Oh, the Places We Went!

One Man's Journey with Alzheimer's and Dementia

Sandy Tomlin

Copyright © 2025 by Sandy Tomlin

All Rights Reserved.

ISBN: 979-8-218-76878-2

To Mom and Dad for establishing such loving and lasting roots

In word and deed, honor your father,
that his blessings may come upon you;
for a father's blessing gives a family firm roots,
... Take care of your father when he is old;
grieve him not as long as he lives.
Even if his mind fail, be considerate with him;...
For kindness to a father will not be forgotten...
It will take lasting root.

Sirach 4:8-9,12-14

Contents

Prologue ix

Do You Hear What I Hear? 1

Jigsaw Puzzle 4

Name Tags 6

Yo Ho Ho! Pirates on the Go! 8

Have You Met My Friend...Whatchacallit 10

There is Something About a Baby 12

Easter Card 14

Can the Boys Come Over? 16

Sprechen Sie Deutsch 18

I'm Not Wearing That! 20

Mowing at the Farm 22

Good Night Gorilla 24

Takeshi 26

Thank Heaven for Answering Machines 28

Back Seat Driver 30

A Joyful Alleluia! 32

You're Not My Brother 34

Honor Flight 36

May 20, 2014 36

Ditty Dot Ditty 41

Sonny 42

Are Those Words Coming From Grandma? 44

- Oops! He Georged it! 46
- That Poor Lampshade 48
- You're Going to Poke Someone's Eye Out! 50
- I Don't Know Who You Are, but I Know I Love You! 51
- I Guess You're Going to Tell Me They're Dead, Too! 53
- Turn Your Shirt Inside Out 54
- What to Wear 57
- Is Your Name Carrot? 59
- No Filters 61
- Zulu Time 63
- Grandma the Great Escape Artist 65
- Computer Games 67
- We Drove 100 Miles for That? 69
- The Fountain of Youth 71
- Back to First Grade 73
- Holy Day of Obligation 77
- Go! Go! Go!…Wrong Team, Dad 79
- Table for One 81
- Bring the Dogs 83
- @*#! Dad's Walking 85
- I Need a Bag Man 87
- Dad and Kathy Sitting on a Swing 89
- Lost and Found 91
- The New Hat 93
- Crossword Anyone? 95

No Touchy	97
Keep Him Busy	99
Charleston Chew	101
Let's Go Look at Christmas Lights	103
Golden Anniversary	105
Pee on the Plane	107
The Night Before Christmas	109
Tootsie	112
Thank God for Comics	114
GPS Directions	116
Did You Have Enough Rubbers?	118
Loved that Silky Feel	119
Is My Mom Dead?	121
Hi, Dad	123
Let's Go Walk the Stores	125
DVR Time	127
What is it About a Shower	129
He Got Out of The Car!	131
Old Time Cartoons	133
How the Hell Did He do That?	134
Who Lives Here?	136
IHOP Friends	138
Chickens in the Freezer	140
Just Like Riding a Bike	142
Dad Loved his Beer	144

Tom is Fishing For Dad	146
Friendly's	148
Weren't You in the Marching Band?	150
Alarm and Padlocks	152
Have You Seen my Dog?	154
Who's the Cute Fat Baby?	156
Pee with the Ladies	157
Music	159
Stevie Baby!	161
Hup 2, 3, 4	163
Sonny's Angels	165
Mother' Day	167
Cracker Jack Ring	169
Epilogue	170
Thank You!	172
References	173

Prologue

    This book is mostly about my father, George Wolf, and some side stories of his mother, Hilda Wolf. Both suffered from Alzheimer's dementia. Not only did they teach us how to be of service to others before our journey began, but we learned even more as our journey with them continued. Since then, we have been asked our input on so many things. We have given out our phone numbers, sat down with many families getting on board and traveling along this road, and showed them points of interest along the way. This book covers many of the questions we get asked.

    My dad was all about service. Service to God, then to family and to country. He and Mom were inspirational and set the example of the ultimate good Samaritan. We have been honored and humbled to witness and be a part of this throughout our lives. It has rubbed off on each of their three children, and on their grandchildren. What a legacy!

This in no way is a "how to" book. It is a "how we" book. How we dealt with the many situations that will, and did come up when dealing with Alzheimer's and Dementia. Everyone deals with it differently, we found going to where they were at the time and enjoying the time we spent with them there was so much easier and more enjoyable than forcing them to spend time with us in our world. Not to mention much more fun! We learned so much we never knew. Stories we never had heard before, often laughing until we cried, howled, then fell off the couch.

Embedded in these journeys or chapters are tidbits, tricks, and timing issues revealed that may be of assistance to some, but it is not a cookie-cutter fit for all. Like anything, read, learn, take what you want, and leave the rest. But above all laugh! My dad was a cut up, and he above all else, would want you to laugh right along with us, as we travel on these trips with him.

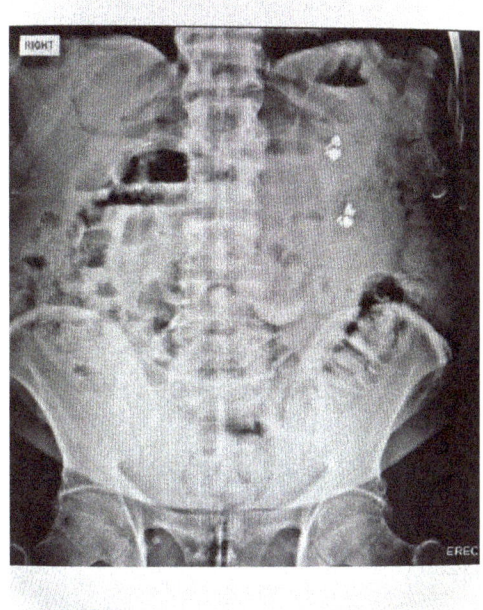

Do You Hear What I Hear?

Late one morning I got a call from my sister in South Carolina. "Banana!" (My nickname) "you'll never believe what Dad did... he swallowed his hearing aids!"

"What!" I exclaimed.

"Yeah, he swallowed them!"

She went on to explain that she and Mom and Dad were sitting at the table, drinking their coffee when Mom looked over and saw Dad was trying very hard to swallow something. She asked him what he just swallowed, and he replied that he took the two big pink pills on the table. Mom said to Deb that she had already given him all his morning pills earlier. Did Deb give him something to eat?

After further questioning, they figured out that those "big pink pills" were his hearing aids. After I got finished belly-laughing, I heard Mom protest in the background, saying,

"I don't find this funny. I am the one who's going to have to go through his poop to make sure they come out." At this point, my sister and I burst into laughter all over again.

Later, I get another phone call. It's my sister, Deb, in the car with my parents, heading to the ER because they were concerned about the batteries in the hearing aids. Before they hung up (we were on speakerphone) I said to my dad to behave for the doctors.

"He can't hear you." Deb reminded me.

"Well put the phone on his stomach!"

When we relayed the story to our brother, Tom he told Mom, that these "two" shall pass! Needless to say, she was not amused. This just made us start laughing all over again, until our stomachs hurt.

Once at the hospital, they x-rayed him and yep, there were two hearing aids. But wait! There's more! There were also two quarters and a dime. My cousin, Gary, made the comment that the government would never look for his money there.

Dad came home and poor Mom had the unenviable task to make sure that he passed both hearing aids with batteries intact. When all was said and done (it took a few days) Mom recovered all but the dime. "Well, that was a shitty tip anyway," Gary quipped. And my husband said, "Mom, you always said he had shit in his ears."

We all had hopes of getting his x-ray with the hearing aids in his stomach to make Christmas cards. We were going to title them: Do You Hear What I Hear?

We all still laugh at the retelling of this story. Even Mom laughs now. She marvels how this happened so quickly and with both she and my sister sitting right there next to him. It was a good thing he did this in front of them, had he done it when no one was around, we still would be looking for those hearing aids. My mom had to undergo another indignity when she had to take the now pooped out, cleaned up hearing aids back to the Veterans Administration Hospital, and explain what happened in order to get replacements. They were incredulous. This was a new one for them as well. They just held up the garbage can for her to put them in. It is my opinion, that this happens more often than people are aware of. After this we were more vigilant of things he put in his mouth and things that we sat down in front of him. Change was not left in front of him or in a dish either. We didn't come out of this experience smelling like a rose – at least not Mom. But as with all of life's lessons, you learn and move on. Grateful that that was all that happened.

Jigsaw Puzzle

My mom and dad went out to my Aunt Dene's house one to two times a week to help clean and do whatever needed doing around the house. They would wash down walls, clean, and even paint. My Aunt Dene always had a jigsaw puzzle set up for my dad to work on while he was there. There were days when he could go right through them and other times he took no interest in them.

My mom also had a jigsaw puzzle set up at home for Dad to work on as well as anyone else who wanted to join in on the fun. Between Mom and Dad they made three very large Thomas Kincade puzzles that took months to complete. Mom decoupaged them and we framed them and they are hanging in my home to this day. People who see them still marvel that 1.) they are puzzles, and 2.) my father was the one who put them together.

Jigsaw puzzles, word finds, crosswords, anything that will challenge the brain is a must to keep the brain active. With this disease in our family history, we are all very aware of the likelihood of our futures.

We make sure we stay on top of things. This includes but is not limited to diet, staying active, regular doctor visits, exercise and things like playing cards, doing jigsaw puzzles, sudoku, crossword puzzles, and word search to mention a few.

Early detection is very important and can really make a difference. For more information consult your physician or the Alzheimer's Association. My siblings and I hope for more of my mom's genes than my father's when it comes down to it, but we are all glad that we got his sense of humor.

Name Tags

There are six grandchildren in our immediate family. The oldest four were born almost in yearly succession. My first came ten years later, then my second arrived three and a half years after him. Three boys and three girls.

As far as grandparents go, my parents are up there with the best! Camping trips, day trips to parks, season passes to Kings Island. When there, if everyone behaved and followed the rules, ice cream was the reward before they left for the day. Making Christmas cookies with Nana and fishing with Paps (or Papa, as the older four grandchildren called him), were both dearly loved and much anticipated.

As Alzheimer's and dementia progressed, as is typical, Dad was forgetting names. He was calling the younger boys the name of the oldest grandson and the girls all looked so similar, it was hard for a lot of people to keep them straight. Their ages went from 14 to 3 at the time so not all of them understood why their grandfather was calling them the incorrect name. The seven year old, then a first grader, made a stellar suggestion.

"If Paps can't remember our names, why don't we wear name tags? That's what we do in school." So, Nana went and got her mailing stickers and made name tags for everyone. Problem solved for that day and a few others as well.

Confusion with names is often typical of people without the diagnosis of Alzheimer's. Several reasons can contribute to this such as being tired, stress or outside distractions. These all can cause confusion and mixed up or forgotten names. However, with Alzheimer's and Dementia it becomes more frequent and evident. We noticed it started with people he didn't see as often or had just met and it progressed.

My son's suggestion to wear name tags really worked well. My dad would stop the kids and they would turn and point to their name tags and all was well with both parties. Of course, Dad would always wink and give them a thumbs up as well.

One other observation worth mentioning. Empowering the grandchildren to make useful suggestions that would help their grandfather have a better day. This simple act of listening and acknowledging, then acting on those suggestions taught all the grandchildren compassion, patience and gentleness.

SANDY TOMLIN

Yo Ho Ho! Pirates on the Go!

Having a family member with Alzheimer's and dementia can be very draining on a family. However, the main caregiver, which often times is the spouse, gets hit the hardest. Living with it 24/7 and constantly being aware of their loved one's movements, even to the point of sleeping with one eye open. It just takes it out of a person.

My siblings and I all did our part to help out, as well as our spouses. One thing my husband and I and our two boys always did was to go out to breakfast every Sunday after going to church with them and at least once during the week we would meet for dinner. On one particular occasion my dad was back in his boyhood days. As we were sitting at a table in a crowded restaurant, he takes his napkin and puts it on his head, grabs his fork and knife and starts acting like a pirate.

My boys were younger then and they loved it. My mom was starting to get upset and embarrassed. So what do we do? We joined him in his boyhood. We grabbed our napkins and put them on our heads! My husband made some corny dad joke about what do you pay a pirate for corn...a buccaneer. Ugh! Of course, he used his best pirate imitation as well. Aaaarrrrggghhh! The waitress knew us and Dad and she joined right in. We had a bountiful night!

This is just one of many examples of things that can, and will happen out in public. Don't be embarrassed by it. Your loved one certainly is not. What they are doing is totally normal and make sense to them.

Join them where they are. Go to the place that they are and enjoy them there. We heard about the Lookout tree and one of the childhood friends he played pirates with.

Sometimes it doesn't work, but we found that for us, it did more often than not. It's always worth a try. It's amazing how most people are understanding if you feel the need to explain.

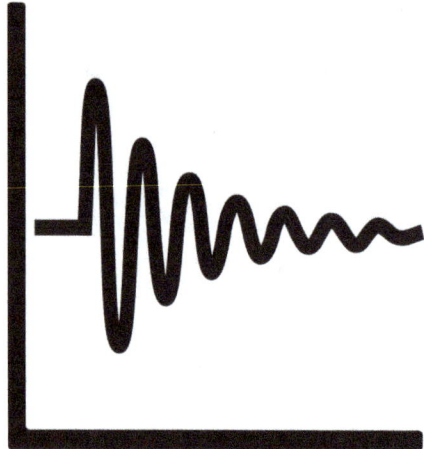

Have You Met My Friend...Whatchacallit

My father had a great way of disguising when he didn't know someone or remember something. To begin with, he was never good with names. So someone named Jerry would be called Gary and so forth.

As his Alzheimer's and dementia progressed, it would become, "Oh, you know whatchacallit." He would snap his fingers as he tried to remember. And that is how he would cover for not being able to recall. It would be the same for when we spoke about where he may have traveled, and we went to that whatchacallit place or ate at Whatchacallit's. He didn't want to look like he didn't remember and he covered it well.

Here are some things we learn to DO and NOT TO DO. One of them not to do was to ask Dad if he knew our names or the name of someone that we were with. It would be an embarrassment and often times it drove home the fact that he had an issue and often that would be upsetting not only for him, but for the family as well.

He would smack his fist into his other hand and shake his head. He knew something was wrong and that he was missing something. We were quick to assure him that everyone forgets things once in a while and not worry about it. We also reminded him that we were right there with him and we wouldn't leave him alone, and he would be just fine.

Another do is just sit quietly until he sees you. Don't barge in and expect him to be happy, especially if he's watching something on TV. or in the middle of doing something. Also don't come from behind and touch. Always try to circle around to the front or call out the name to let them know that you are right there. You want to see a fight or flight reflex? You'll get one, and it may not be the one you want.

There is Something About a Baby

So soothing and soft, smells so good – most of the time. A baby is just a miracle and can work miracles. When we had adopted our oldest son, the other four grandchildren ranged in age from 10 to 14 years old. Three and a half years later our youngest came along. They came at the perfect time interval for my dad. He loved nothing more than to spend time with his grandchildren. The other four were growing up and it wasn't easy to do things together. Then along comes Ben, just when Dad's Alzheimers and dementia was starting to show. He would hold Ben, feed him, sing to him and talk to him.

Dad was a member of the Veterans of Foreign Wars, American Legion and Disabled American Veterans. he was on the color guard and he also was the chaplain. Dad could say all the prayers by heart at all of the Memorial Day and Veterans Day celebrations. Dad sold poppies every year and we made it a point to always go see him and buy our poppies from him. He was Poppy King several years in a row.

We always went to watch Dad march in the Memorial Day Parade. A fond memory we have is of three-year-old Ben, running out to see his Paps as he marched by. Then he stayed out there with his grandfather and walk the rest of the parade with him. Holding Paps' hand and 'marching' along side of him.

Then Nate came along just as Ben was starting preschool and Dad had another baby to hold and sing to talk to and love. His doctor at the time, said he wished he had a Ben and Nate for all of his Alzheimer's and dementia patients.

As it happens, Dad had five more babies to love on. Two were his great grandsons Kristopher and Xavier. Both lived in South Carolina and were born within two years of each other. Those boys really kept him occupied when Mom and Dad went down to visit.

The other three belong to a good friend of mine, Eva, Lily and Maddie, triplets! I went over once a week for close to two years to help out. We called it "triplet duty" and loved every second of it. Every so often I would take Dad with me. I'd sit him down and put a baby in his arms and sit next to him and fold laundry. If that baby got restless, I just exchanged it for another one and so on.

It was a great system. My friend got much needed rest. I was able to get some things done for her and Dad and I both got to love on those babies.

Please note: my father was never left alone with one of the many babies described above. We were always right there beside him ready to take over in a moments notice.

It is very important that you never leave and Alzheimer's and dementia patient alone with children, especially babies and little ones. They often don't know their strengths and the last thing they want to do is hurt them, so you need to be right there to make sure that doesn't happen. It also is frustrating to a person with Alzheimer's and dementia, to be told "no" by a 3-year-old. So again, it is very important that you are right there to intervene, and make sure that nothing happens.

My father now has a third great grandson, Emmett, he gets to watch over and love on him from heaven.

Easter Card

If you don't take your loved ones out because they have Alzheimer's and dementia and you don't want to be embarrassed by them, you are really missing out. I'm sure you did plenty as a kid that turned their faces red as you embarrassed them. The point is, there's no reason to be embarrassed. You are enjoying time with your loved ones, and they absolutely are as well. Granted, there may come a time when you may not be able to take your loved one out, but while you can, I encourage you to take full advantage of it.

Point in fact. We always did an Easter brunch with my grandmother, our family and my uncle's family. One year we were at a nice place for brunch. I had given Grandma an Easter card, she read it, thanked me and put it in her pocket. A little while later she found the card in her pocket, took it out, read it, told me how beautiful it was, and put it back in her pocket.

We all knew then what was coming, so we put down guesses as to how many times she would read that card during our 2-to-3 hour brunch. Guesses started out in the 20's and went up from there. I said 85. The point was to be the closest without going over. I won. Final count 84!

Some may think this was cruel, but there was absolutely no malice intended. At no time was Grandma aware of what we were doing. It started out as a way of passing the time for the kids. But more importantly, 84 times that day my grandmother smiled and knew she was loved. How special is that!

Can the Boys Come Over?

Grandchildren are a blessing in more ways than one. By the time Dad started to really show signs, the older four grandchildren were preteen, and two of them lived in South Carolina.

When our oldest came along in 1999 it was a blessing for all. Dad always wanted to be the one to take care of him. He would take him for walks. They would sit out on the street corner and watch the big trucks go by. They called them "Big Beauties" He had Dad's complete attention for 3 1/2 years. Then our youngest came along and we were twice Blessed. Dad could give his attention to the baby and Ben could continue to grow in independence.

Dr. Steve, again marveled at the benefits that were bestowed upon Dad and wished he had a Ben and Nate for all of his Alzheimer's and Dementia patients. As the boys grew to toddler, preschool and beyond, they loved going over to Nana and Paps' house. Sometimes Mom would call to ask if the boys could come over so Dad could play cars with them. There is a lake behind their condo that we had stocked with fish when they moved in. He and Mom would take the boys out and fish with frozen hot dogs for bait. So many wonderful memories and a great stress relief for Mom.

Please be smart. I can't stress enough that you cannot leave your kids alone with a person with Alzheimer's and dementia. Someone needs to be within arms' reach at all times. Still, it does take some pressure off the main caregiver when they can watch the people they love have fun together.

Sometimes we would stay and send Mom out to shop or do whatever for a while. She rarely took us up on this opportunity. She always had Dad go with her to the stores and push the cart.

SANDY TOMLIN

Sprechen Sie Deutsch

Most of my dad's family were all descendants from Germany as were my mom's. So he grew up speaking a smattering of German and also learned more while in high school. My dad went into the Air Force when he was 17 years old and landed in Germany on his 18th birthday. He was stationed there for a little more than three years.

He often spoke phrases to us as we were growing up and when one of us was born, he would call my mom's mom and give her all the information speaking German. He did this because they were on a party line and not all the neighbors on the line could understand German. (For those who don't know what a party line is, as late as the 1960's, neighbors shared a telephone line. Each household would have its own unique ring; my grandparents' was 3 rings in a row. You would then know the call was for you, so you should pick up your receiver. In the evenings or winter, when there wasn't much happening, the neighbors picked up their receivers, too. Therefore, everyone knew the business of their neighbors-a party line indeed!).

As his Alzheimer's and dementia progressed, his use of certain phrases in German increased. So any new comers to the family had to learn phrases such as "Mach die tur zu bitte" or "Wie spät ist es?" In English, "close the door please" and "what time is it?" Trust me, there were plenty of other phrases we learned as well, but those will not be printed here.

I heard an analogy one time about having Alzheimer's and what happens to the short term memory versus that of someone not afflicted with this disease. I wish that I could remember (uh oh) who said it so I could give proper credit. Essentially, it went something like this.

If you had a drawer and you put all your short term memories into it, you would be able to come back to that drawer, open it and retrieve those memories. A person with Alzheimer's can put their short-term memories into a drawer, but this drawer doesn't have a bottom so all the memories fall through and therefore, can't be retrieved.

What we experienced with both my father and my grandmother, was that not only the short term memories fell through, but overtime other memories fell in as well and were lost or distorted. I encourage you to keep as much of those memories alive for as long as you can. When that doesn't work, make new ones.

Dad and Grandma

I'm Not Wearing That!

My grandmother loved to be in style and always wore clothes that represented what was in vogue at the time. When she was placed into the nursing facility, as so often happens, her clothes would disappear. Whether it was another patient coming into her room and thinking the clothes were theirs or the unfortunate disappearance without a clue, but shrouded in suspicion.

Grandma would be given other clothes to wear and she let it be known under no uncertain terms that she did not like the choices given to her, they did not suit her and definitely were not to her liking. She was pretty vocal about how she was not about to wear that!

This would prompt a call from the nursing home to my parents that more clothes were needed because Grandma would not get dressed. My mom and dad couldn't keep buying her new clothing, so my mom, being a seamstress, bought inexpensive sweat suits and decorated them up with material and buttons to look fashionable.

Another thing that helped was that Mom started doing Grandma's laundry. If there were nice clothes for certain occasions she would keep those at home and not send them back. Instead we would take them over and have her change into them before we went somewhere. Also, she sewed Grandma's name onto all of her clothing. She sewed it on with such a fine stitch that it would be a pain and possibly rip a hole in the material to remove the tag. She also put the name on the outside of the garments. It became very easy to spot a "whoopsie" borrower that way. As a last resort, Mom started using sharpies to write her name on her clothing.

One thing to note-

Pay attention to issues with dressing. A lot of times gym suits or sweat shirts are not easy to pull over one's head or to raise their arms above their head to get the garment on. Likewise arthritic hands can have issues with buttons and zippers. Help your loved one out whether at home or a facility and find clothing that is easy and comfortable for them to wear.

Mowing at the Farm

My dad loved to drive, and when he could no longer drive, my brother, Tom, came up with the idea of letting him drive the small, riding mower out at his place in the country. There he allowed him to mow the grass in certain areas. Dad was happy as a clam. This worked out well, but as his condition progressed my sister-in-law and brother watched him closer when he mowed.

At one point, he veered from the area they had given him to mow. All of a sudden they saw all this debris flying in the air as he went over areas that had more than just grass to mow. One of them stayed in the area he was mowing and kept directing him at that point.

Another time, and probably the final time he mowed, Dad decided he had to urinate. What he did was stop the tractor, but didn't set the brake or turn the tractor off. He then climbed off the tractor in order to do so. There was a mad dash to get to him.

Riding lawnmowers, have operator-presence controls, or seat switches, which kills the motor, and stalls it out if the operator comes off the seat. Once again, they were right there to take care of the situation and it was decided that Dad's mowing days were finished.

He would ask Tom when they were going to go mowing again, and Tom would give him a vague or redirecting answer, like "I just did it over the weekend," kind of answer. There were plenty of other little things that Tom found for he and Dad to work on. Often Mom and Dad would be invited to just spend several days with them enjoying the country. Overtime, Dad forgot about the mowing and Tom was careful not to do it when our parents were invited out.

Good Night Gorilla

Our youngest son, Nathan, and my dad had a very unique and special relationship. Nate had apraxia, and was unable to speak his first words until after 2-years-old. We did sign language with him, though his brother Ben was the one who could understand him best.

My dad, however, knew what it was like to not be understood. Around that time, I had a tension fracture in my back and was bed bound. My parents took the kids from 8 PM until Rich got home at 3 PM the next day. We would all eat together, Rich would spend time with the boys and they would take off at bedtime.

Every day at nap time and bedtime, my dad would read stories to Nate. Nate would almost always pick out the book *Good Night Gorilla*. I don't know what the draw to this book was, but, if I had to guess I would guess it was how Dad read the book. He would put in all the sounds and motions of the animals, the squeaks, and the knocks. I'm not sure, but I think Nate was able to imitate the sounds with Dad, but at least he could mirror the motions. Whatever it was, it brought about a special bond only the two of them shared.

Mom still has the original book and it will go to Nate when the time comes. Until then, every new baby, whether it's family, friend, or teacher, who has a baby gets *Good Night Gorilla* with a synopsis of why it's such a special book. They are invited to make it their own with new noises and hand motions.

It was just so special to see the two of them curled up with this book. Nate on Dad's lap listening intently. Nate didn't like to be held or cuddled as a baby or toddler but, when it came to this book and Dad he was riveted. So so special!

Takeshi

When Dad was first diagnosed with Alzheimer's and dementia, my husband had a work assignment in Japan. After a month, I was able to go and join him. We talked my parents into going and seeing Japan, Australia and New Zealand.

On our second day in Japan. Mom, Dad and I set out to see the shops in the city of Kobe. I was trying to find picture postcards to send home, but, couldn't quite get the message across in translation. A young teenager approached us and offered his service as a translator to help us. This was how we met Takeshi. Not only did he help us find postcards, but also took us to the post office, where he helped us purchase the correct postage.

When we returned to our hotel that afternoon, there was a message inviting us to dinner at his family's home. We couldn't believe it! Our second day there and we were invited to eat a traditional meal with a Japanese family! When we arrived at their home, the next day, Dad had some trouble with the shoe and slipper exchange, but we got through that. Takeshi was our interpreter between his parents and us. His mom had made a delicious stew with hard-boiled eggs in it, and we all laughed so hard at poor Dad, trying to eat that egg with chopsticks.

Oh, the Places We Went!

That summer, Takeshi, then 16 years old, came to America and stayed with my parents for three weeks. We took him all around: Amish country to see the sunflower fields and Washington D.C., he especially wanted to see the Lincoln Memorial.

Twice more Takeshi came and stayed with my parents through the years and he became part of our family.

When Takeshi learned of my father's passing, he called and we all talked with him. He then called back and asked if it would be too much if he flew in for my dad's funeral. Takeshi flew coach arrived Friday-in time for the visitation. He told us he would not be the man he had become without the influence of my father. He honored us by agreeing to be a pallbearer for Dad, something we all knew Dad would have loved, as the rest were grandchildren and neph-ew. Takeshi then flew back to Japan Sunday afternoon.

If that wasn't enough to show you the love between Takeshi and my parents, maybe this will be. We had one family member, not an immediate family member but close, who told my mom that he and his family couldn't make my father's funeral because they had reservations for a trip they had planned. We all understood that life can sometimes get in the way. We later learned it was reservations to a campground just 45 minutes away for the weekend. They very easily could have come to the funeral or at least the visitation. We were very disheartened when we found out the lie we had been told. We are choosing to think that maybe it was just too much for him to be there and that was the way he covered it. Here Takeshi drops everything and flies for 20 hours one way to be there with us and then flies back 36 hours later. It's all about priorities and love. Takeshi's love and respect for Dad and Mom is a beautiful gift to our family. One that we will always cherish.

Thank Heaven for Answering Machines

Believe it or not, there was a time when there was no such thing as a cell phone or an answering machine. Phones were tethered to the wall with a box and a telephone cord coming off of that to a handset. This meant, unless you had a long and stretched out cord, you were stuck in the kitchen, talking in front of everyone present.

When my grandmother was first placed in the nursing care facility, the one thing she remembered was our phone number and she would call it constantly. Probably every time she walked by a phone she would pick it up and dial. Of course, you had to pick the phone up and answer it because you didn't know who was calling and it could be important.

"Oh hi Grandma."

"No, it hasn't been that long since we last talked."

"Really?! Well, I'll try and do better."

And so it went, sometimes 30 to 40 times a day. No sense in telling her you just talked to her 10 times just within the last two hours, she'd tell you just how wrong you were in no uncertain terms. So you just went with the flow, apologized for being bad about not calling her and that you would do better.

This started the routine of the "Ask and Answer" game. Everyone that was in earshot of the conversation knew all the questions that were coming and how they would be answered. Sometimes we played the part of Grandma, voice imitation included, and other times that of the lucky one answering the phone.

My mom was so excited when she got an answering machine. She could screen the calls and answer maybe one out of 10 calls from Grandma. My dad worked third shift so he was delighted to get some sleep during the day.

Cell phones, yep, you'll still get the calls. And yeah, you can turn off unwanted calls. I think they can remember your number and it gives them comfort, knowing they can remember something. Some normalcy if you will, and getting to hear the voice of a loved one on the other end, that has to be reassuring as well.

Please, I know it can be a pain, but don't go out of your way to dodge those calls. Think instead of how your voice may be reassuring them, and settling them down. Put yourself in their shoes. Now, ask yourself, would you like someone to say, "Hello?"

Back Seat Driver

Oh my gosh! Have you ever had a backseat, front seat, back third row seat, driver? Then you have never had the pleasure of driving my dad around. That duty usually fell to my mom or me if I was with them or taking Dad out to stores with me. But next in line had to be my husband.

We would go on family outings and take my parents along in our van. At first we put Dad up front with Rich so he could see the scenery. If you could imagine a long journey where EVERY sign you passed, being read out loud, and if it was an exit sign, Rich would be asked if that was the exit we needed to take.

So then we moved him to the backseat. Problem solved, or so we thought. He quit reading the signs, but then he could look over Rich's shoulder and see the dashboard. "What's the speed limit?

You might be going too fast."

"Hey, you're down to half a tank of gas. Don't you think we should fill up?"

And so on.

OK that didn't work. Let's move him to the third row and see what happens.

"It's feeling a little bumpy back here. Maybe we should pull off and check your tires."

We finally figured out the only place that worked, was the seat where he closed his eyes and went to sleep.

Yes. This can get on your nerves especially if you're the driver. We always tried to divert his attention until the next round started. Some days were better than others. We did lots of laughing because really, what else can you do?

There's no sense getting angry or frustrated. It is what it is. During tense times, like bad weather, we would shush him and tell him he had to be quiet because the driver needed to concentrate. That he understood and did comply with, for the most part.

A Joyful Alleluia!

Catholic mass. If you are Catholic, you go to mass a minimum of once a week. Of course, as a child, you didn't always understand what an amazing blessing it is to attend mass and receive the body, blood, soul and divinity of Christ. But as you grow and learn and study the prayers, you can say by route, they actually become a type of a love poem, given to us by Christ. This gives us hope, faith and nourishment.

The symbolism that incorporates the Old and New Testament is beautifully scripted, and demonstrates the love and power of the Holy Trinity, as we witness the transubstantiation of bread and wine to the consecrated body and blood of Christ.

This was everything for Dad. He knew the Latin prayers by heart, and then, when it switched to English, he knew all of the prayers and professed them loudly, and proudly. In later years, they once against changed some of the wording for more clarity and better understanding. Poor Dad just couldn't get the new changes down. He loudly and proudly still recited the original English prayers. There is a family that sits in the pew in front of us on Saturdays.

The parents and the young boys would have big wide grins on their faces, and sometimes little giggles would slip out as Dad would recite the old prayers.

    Thankfully, there were missalettes at church for people to follow along. We could usually get him to follow along as we pointed out the prayers to him. This helped him say the correct words for the prayers. As always, it was a joyful alleluia.

You're Not My Brother

My dad's younger brother's name is Bill. He's eight years younger than Dad-almost to the day. As a boy, Dad spent a lot of time around Bill and often times caring for Bill. So it stands to reason that they did many things together.

When Bill came over to the house on holidays or to celebrate their birthdays, Dad wouldn't always recognize him. The mustache and glasses would throw him for a loop. And he would voice his concerned that he didn't believe that Bill was his brother. Bill would sit with him and tell him how they would go sled riding down the hill at the Jewish Hospital, or go to their aunt and uncle's houses or farms, Dad would remember those things and start talking about them with Bill.

If someone or some thing, interrupted their conversation, Dad might revert back to not knowing Bill once again. Bill would patiently start over again from the beginning.

It takes time and patience when dealing with those with Alzheimer's and dementia. Be willing to dig deep into past memories and try to get there with them. It is a good bet that you won't get them to present day memories because they just don't have those anymore. Figuring out where they are and traveling down that road to meet up with them is usually your best bet. What Bill did was very smart. Knowing what they did as children and bringing up those childhood memories that Dad could remember was ingenious. Dad was able to latch onto those and get with Bill and they were able to have nice conversations and laugh about friends that they once knew.

Honor Flight
May 20, 2014

What an honor! Dad was selected to go on an honor flight. Unfortunately, my brother Tom had just had shoulder surgery so he was unable to go with dad and spouses are not to go along on this trip. So Mom asked Rich if he would do the honors, which he was more than happy to do.

On the morning of May 20, 2014 the wake up call came at 3:20 AM. We had to be at Greater Cincinnati Northern Kentucky International Airport by 6 AM. They would be boarding a charter flight to Washington DC with 71 other veterans that flew with their guardian. Two of them were World War II veterans.

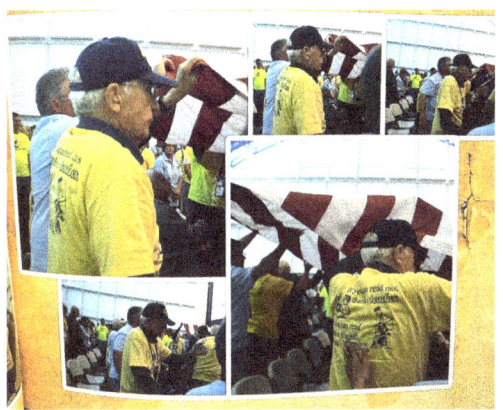

Mom, Ben, Nathan and myself accompanied them for their sendoff. There was great fanfare, as there was a color guard, drum and bagpipe corp that marched the veterans in to start the day. There were speeches of gratitude, and Mr. Ed Fink stood up and had a flag in his hands. He unfurled that flag and he said that this flag was going be taken to the World War II monument and each veteran was to proudly touch this flag because it was going to be flown over that monument.

He then read a poem about the American flag.

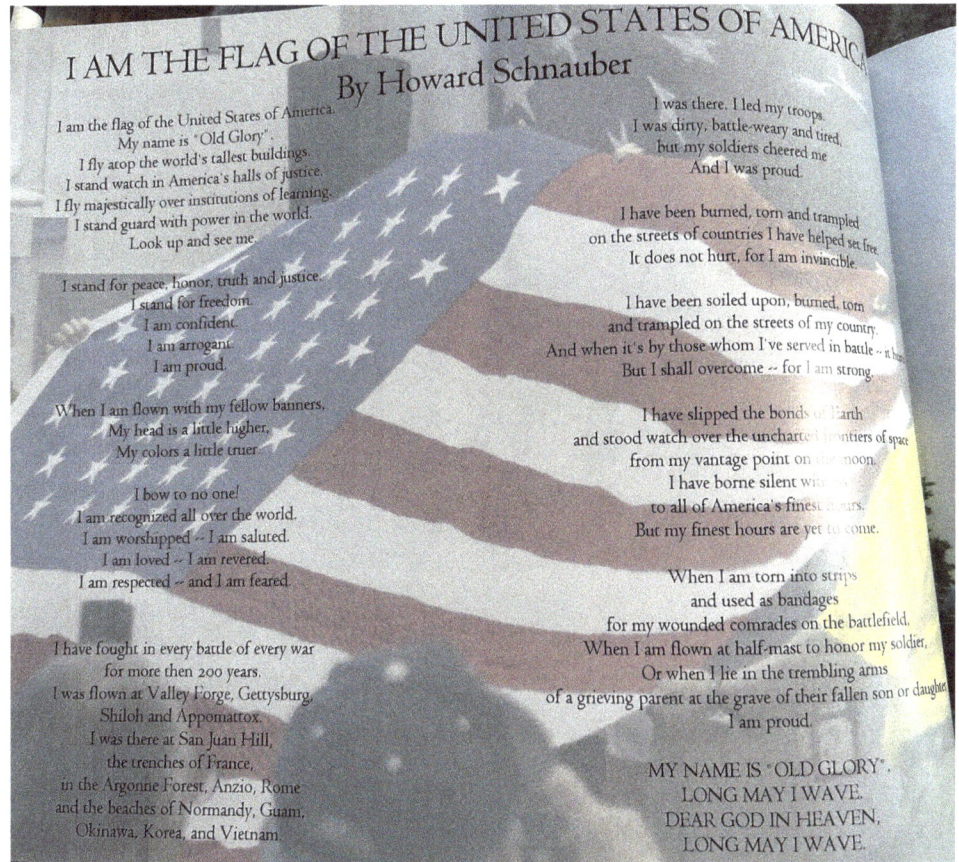

Fire trucks were there on takeoff and landing, giving the veterans a water cannon salute! There also was a color guard on the tarmac and as the plane got ready for take-off, there was a rainbow in the sky.

A police escort was there for the three luxury buses to the Iwo Jima Monument. Rich had to do some fast talking here to get Dad into a wheelchair. He finally appealed to Dad's sense of fairness when he said to just sit in it so that we aren't slowing people down. "Once we get there you can get up and walk around." That did the trick, Dad climbed aboard, and away they went.

Other monuments visited: Tomb of the Unknown Soldier, Air Force Memorial, Korean Conflict, Lincoln Monument and the World War II Memorial.

When it was time for them to eat, Dad didn't want to get off the bus he was tired. So Rich made up some story about how they had to clean the bus and he couldn't stay on the bus while they cleaned the bus. So they got off the bus and he went into the hall and he got something to eat.

All of the servicemen also got Certificates of Commendation from Senators Rob Portman and Sherrod Brown. They also got letters of thanks written to them by different school children.

Thankfully the chaperones, for lack of a better word, of the trip were versed in how to handle veterans with different issues. So if there was a problem, they could quickly handle or assist the guardians in handling a veteran if the need arose. There was no need on this particular trip. It was a very smooth and well done operation.

Rich and Dad waiting for the flight home.

When the veterans came home, they were greeted once again with the ladder trucks and the water cannons. They had the drum and bugle corps, and they had women dressed up as pinup girls, and they gave each veteran a bag of kisses as they came in to the airport. The flag was the first to follow the honor guard then came the veterans. There were people there 11:30 at night with banners and flags cheering all the veterans on. The man in front of us, when he got to his wife said to her, "When I came home from Vietnam it was just my parents at the train station. I'm finally home!" My brother, Tom, my mom, myself and our two sons, Nathan and Benjamin, were there to greet Rich and Dad as they walked in. What a day it was for them perfect in every way.

Sandy Tomlin

Honor Flight Mission
We offer honor flights to veterans so they may visit their
memorials in Washington, D. C.
All World War II, Korean War and Vietnam War veterans age 65 and older,
Who served either stateside or overseas are eligible.
We will leave **No One** behind!
HonorFlight.Org If you are interested in being an honor flight guardian or sponsor,
you can find details on the national website at honorflight.org

Over 6000 veterans from the Cincinnati area have been able to go on this trip of a lifetime. To donate go to the website at

www.honorflighttri-state.org
or send check or money order to:
Honor Flight Tri-state, 8627 Calumet Way, Cincinnati OH 45249.

Ditty Dot Ditty

My dad's job in the Air Force was radio operator. He knew Morse Code forward and backward. In fact, when he was finished in Germany, he taught the new recruits Morse Code and how to use the radio. Dad always taught us SOS in case we were ever in an emergency we could signal it. As he got older, what is not unusual with Alzheimer's and dementia patients, is he could remember the code, even if he couldn't remember what happened five minutes ago.

It was one of my boys' birthdays and for fun we asked Dad if he could say happy birthday in the ditty dot ditty language. Without missing a beat, he rattled off happy birthday, and at the end either Ben or Nate, was added flawlessly. It was so impressive.

Try it yourself. Dashes equal ditties and dots or periods equal dots.

H .... A .- P .--. P .--. Y -.--

B -... I .. R .-. T – H .... D -.. A .- Y-.--

Not so easy is it?

It never ceased to amaze us the things he remembered without failure or error. Just so impressive.

Sonny

49 years! Wow! Mom and Dad were married 49 years and we celebrated it in Germany. Rich had to go to Germany for work and my dad had never been back since he was stationed there with the Air Force. So Mom, Dad and I went along for a week.

Once again, we took off while Rich had to work. Of course, everything had changed, and his old place where he was stationed was no more. It was sad to see. However, when we went to the town and a little bar/restaurant/theater that he used to go to was still there, Georg's. We went inside, and Dad was talking and remembering things and pointing things out. The lady behind the counter heard him say the name, "Sonny" and she inquired about it. Dad said that when he was there, she was a snot nose little 13-year-old that bit his finger. But they share the same nickname. As luck would have it she was Sonny's daughter, and Sonny was in the other room!

They showed us around and to Dad the place looked the same. Then Sonny pulled out a bottle of cognac, we all had a toast about old friendships.

Dad was about nine years into his Alzheimer's and dementia diagnosis, but his German was as sharp as ever. He was able to communicate with many people and read the menus as well.

We are so happy we made the effort to take him back to see the place where he spent three years of his life. And what an added bonus to once again see Sonny and meet her daughter. It was a treasured experience.

Sonny Georg 1950

SANDY TOMLIN

Are Those Words Coming From Grandma?

When my grandmother was first in the process of being diagnosed with Alzheimer's and dementia, we found a wonderful internist that specialized in this. As it so happened my sister and I both worked with him at the hospital he interned at so we both knew him pretty well.

My grandmother was one of his first patients in his newly formed practice. I went along with my mom when she took her there for her first visit. When Dr. Steve was administering the test to diagnose the degree of her affliction, words started coming out of her mouth that I had never heard her say before. My grandmother was always a well put together lady. As beautiful on the outside, as well as on the inside. Never ever did she use THOSE kind of words! We were shocked and embarrassed for her. Dr. Steve explained that that will happen sometimes when frustration hits. She didn't like the questions he was asking her and deflected with anger and made sure he knew it.

Often times people with Alzheimer's, and dementia will become combative and aggressive. You can't take this personally, there usually is a reason for it, and most often, in our experience, the reason was fear. Fear of not understanding. Fear of not knowing what was going on or where they were going. Sometimes the fear of not knowing who they were with or just fear. Other times it is a part of the disease process. We were lucky in that we could work around my grandmother in order to keep the outburst at bay and even luckier that my father never really experienced these outbursts.

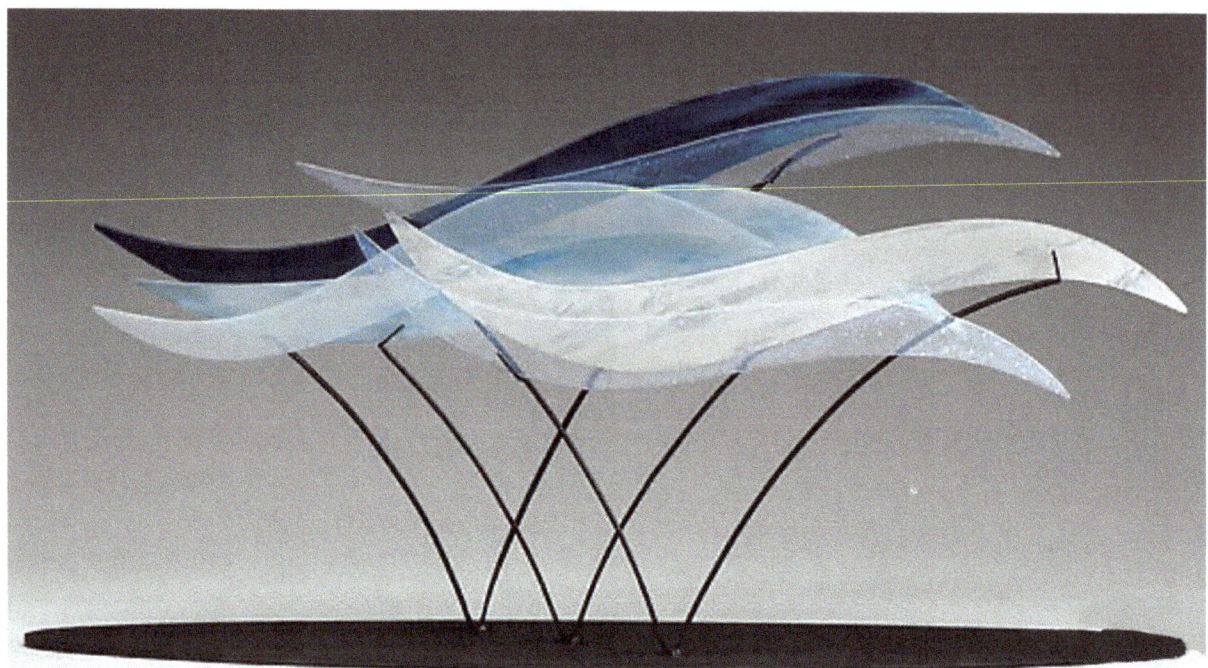

Oops! He Georged it!

My dad did not have the Midas touch. If anything, whatever he touched was certainly going to get dropped, broken or both. This is something he was always known for, always dropping breaking or over tightening things. It got to the point where we would say, "Oops! I Georged it."

He worked for the General Electric Co. for over 40 years, and he had worked himself up to Engine Test. When we would fly and we would hear that they had General Electric engines on the plane we knew that it was a possibility that my dad had tested those engines. We always said to each other that if it survived Dad it's a pretty damn good engine!

These type of things don't go away just because a person is diagnosed with Alzheimer's and dementia. On the contrary, you may see it begin, or even worsen because of it. Mom was upset one day because the glass blown Sydney Opera House she got, when in Australia, was broken. Dad wanted to see it, picked it up and oops, he Georged it.

When people ask us, "What is the first thing you would do if you found out your loved one had Alzheimer's and Dementia?" We always answer, "Put your valuables and things you don't want broken or lost away." It is inevitable that it is going to happen. Somethings are going to get broken. Somethings are going to get lost. So put away valuable things you don't want lost or broken, set things that mean a lot to you out of eyesight if you you don't want to put them away or they will get broken or lost. It's as easy as that.

It is not done on purpose or out of malice. It just happens. It is a fact of life. Things get knocked over, dropped and broken. They get Georged!

That Poor Lampshade

There is a lampshade at my mom's house that sits on the table between the two recliners that Mom and Dad sat in. That poor lampshade, which once was a thing of beauty, is now busted up and torn. There is absolutely no way it will ever get replaced. Here's why:

On many occasions, my dad would, you guessed it, George it. The lamp would be the target that took the brunt of these times. He would set a drink down, put his chair back, pick up a book or the comics, and there went the lamp and the lamp shade.

One evening my parents were sitting watching TV and Mom noticed that Dad was fiddling with his hearing aids. He did this quite often, taking them out, blowing the "dust" out of them, making sure they were on, and finally putting them back in his ears. On this particular occasion he had them out and she saw him pick up his drink. "Oh no! We are not going through that again!" She was remembering the time at my sister's house when he swallowed his hearing aids. She jumped up and demanded that he spit them out. That was not happening. So she grabbed a coaster and pushed it in between his teeth so he couldn't bite her. Yelling at him to open his mouth up wider so she could get her fingers in there. No way was he going to comply and over went the lamp and shade. It got crushed a little more as she stood behind his chair, determined to get the hearing aids out before he swallowed them. Anyone walking by hearing this would have thought that they were hearing the soundtrack to a soft porn movie.

Mom won that round, the poor lampshade lost, and we all had another great laugh, and story to tell.

As I mentioned earlier, that lampshade is still there. Mom won't get rid of it, and we don't want her to either. In fact, we are all hoping we get to have that poor lampshade passed down to us. It carries so many memories, stories and reminders of Dad. It's priceless!

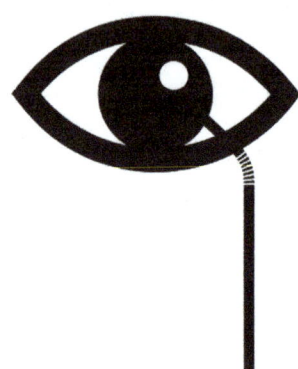

You're Going to Poke Someone's Eye Out!

You're going to poke someone's eye out! This was Dad's mantra when we would sit down in a restaurant and blow the paper off the straws at each other. "Oh, Dad, it's just paper." Then he'd say, "Just wait. One of these times you are not going to be so lucky." We would all laugh, and then he would usually crack a smile after a bit.

If Mom couldn't get Dad to eat or if he was having a bad day, she would take him to a restaurant or have us meet her at one. Thus began the ritual of the straws. It gave Mom a chance to get out of the house and with family around to help keep Dad occupied (like with straw paper shots) it gave her a chance to relax as well. To this day, my family still continues blasting straw paper at each other, in fond remembrance of my dad.

Sometimes, something so easy as going out to eat can be such a pressure reducer for a caregiver. It changes the scenery, you get to take your loved one out for a ride and enjoy a nice meal either together, or with family. Just be careful that "you don't poke someone's eye out!"

I Don't Know Who You Are, but I Know I Love You!

There always comes that first time when your loved one with Alzheimer's and dementia doesn't know you, and it HURTS BAD! The first time I got a Christmas card from Grandma that said, "Love, Aunt Hilda" I cried. So in a very small way, I knew the pain my mom felt the first time my dad didn't know her. It must've cut like a knife. Over 60 years of marriage and he doesn't know who she is.

The strange thing is, though, he knew his feelings for her. He asked her who she was, and she told him her name, and that she was his wife. He thought about that and then said, "I don't know who you are… But I know I love you. So, I think we should get married."

Mom called me later, tears in her voice as she relayed the story to me. I felt so much pain for her, but our family always was taught to look for the bright side of things. So, I asked her if she accepted? Heck, if he keeps asking her, she could get a ring for every finger, toe, and even her navel! By then we were both laughing, and she said she hadn't thought about that.

This is a stark reality. There is going to be a time when your loved one isn't going to know who you are. We found out that it is better not to question them. "Do you know my name?" or "do you know who this is?" Just aren't questions that you want to ask. It just gets them embarrassed and frustrated. For that brief moment, they may become aware that they should know something that they don't.

Just go with the flow. Re-introduced yourself but don't push or make a point of saying that they are incorrect or worse yet, "don't you remember?" My mom was often called Aunt Marie or Aunt Connie, my dad's aunts. You'll have more fun going to the place that they are and you may be surprised at some of the things you may learn along the way.

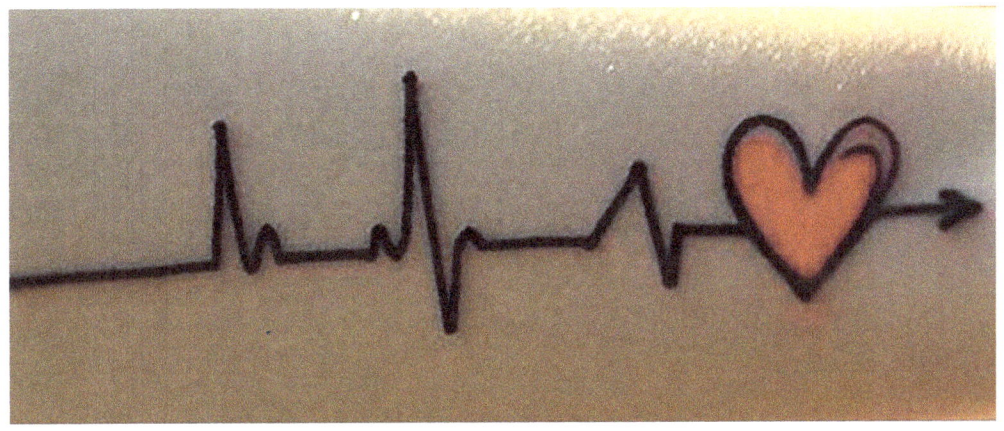

I Guess You're Going to Tell Me They're Dead, Too!

Early on, as we were learning how to deal with Alzheimer's and dementia with Grandma, we fell into the bad habit of talking about her as if she weren't there. We were taking my grandma out for a ride and to dinner. As we were waiting for our food. She asked my mom about her older sister, Marie, and her husband, Ralph. They have been dead for many years, but Grandma refused to believe it, and my mom kept trying to convince her that they were. I finally said to my mom, "Why are you doing that? You're just making her sad and for what so she can go through it again in 10 minutes?"

We changed the subject, and somehow one of Grandma's other sisters came in to the conversation. It was Connie, who died of cancer about 25 years earlier. Grandma asked where she was and my mom, picking her words, said that she wasn't with us today. Grandma looked at my mom and said, "Oh, I suppose you're going to tell me she's dead, too!"

Yes, they hear you. And on a good day, they can hear just enough to put it together and put you in your place.

Please be mindful of what, where, and how you say things in front of and around people with Alzheimer's and dementia. We were able to smile at our little conversation, but I can see where things could be overheard, misunderstood, and that leading to anger and frustration. It just doesn't have to be. If you're careful it won't.

SANDY TOMLIN

Turn Your Shirt Inside Out

As a family, we take a yearly weekend trip around Thanksgiving and head out to my brother and sister-in-law's place in Indiana. We have made many memories there, fried lots of turkeys, dropped a few too, and had many fun times. One of the most memorable involved my niece, Jennifer.

As we were sitting at the table enjoying our Thanksgiving meal, my dad looked across the table and saw Jennifer sitting there. He then noticed her sweatshirt that had a saying on it about nursing. Now, my father rarely, if ever, could pass up reading a sign or sweatshirt, T-shirt... Well, you get the picture. So, he read her saying out loud as usual. "Oh, are you a nurse?"

"I'm going to nursing school to become one" Jenn replies.

"My Aunt Connie was a great nurse!" He says.

"Yes, Papa, I know."

Jennifer answers and excuses herself to get another helping of the deep-fried turkey.

Jennifer sat down and this, of course draws Dad's attention. So he reads her shirt, saying it out loud as usual.

"Oh, are you a nurse?"

"I'm going to school to become one." Jenn replies.

"My Aunt Connie was a great nurse!" he says.

"Yes, Papa, I know."

We all have a small chuckle at Jenn's expense and continue with the meal then someone asks for something to be passed, it went right in front of Jennifer. Yep, that's all it took. He reads the saying out loud,

"Oh, are you going to be a nurse?"

"I'm going to school to become one" Jenn replies.

"My Aunt Connie was a great nurse!"

"Yes, Papa, I know." Jenn answers.

This time we start to giggle. Next time we are slapping our hands on the table to keep from laughing out loud. By the next episode, we are asking the questions and saying the answers right along with them.

Poor Jenn, she's getting flustered by this point. Suddenly she gets up from the table and goes into the restroom. We all look at each other with concern. Oh no, how could we have gotten his mind off of this? Is Jenn in the restroom upset? By that she comes out with a smile on her face, like the cat who ate the canary. She has taken her sweatshirt off, turned it inside out and put it on backwards. She proudly exclaims to the rest of the family, "Note to self, do not wear shirts with words on them around Papa!" We all applauded her creativity.

There certainly are times when dealing with someone with Alzheimer's and dementia can be exasperating. Jennifer showed great restraint in not getting upset and using her creativity to come up with something that would work. Our family chose to look for the good in things and to find the humor in things that was our release. It was something Dad and Mom always taught us, something that's ingrained in us and something that gets us through with a smile every day.

What to Wear

While getting ready to go for an outing, my mom asked my dad to go change his clothes. He did so with no issues, but, he came out wearing a dress shirt with tie, shorts, dress socks, and gym shoes. In his mind, he looked quite dapper, not so with my mom. We now had an issue.

Anyone who has a loved one with Alzheimer's and dementia can tell you getting them to do something they don't want to do or don't think they should have to do, they will dig their heels in hard! My father was no exception. Thankfully my mom got in line twice when God was giving out common sense, and she realize where she went wrong. I can't remember where we were going, but Dad went dressed as he was. Mom told him to get dressed, and he did. Her mistake.

After much discussion, we figured out ways to get Dad to wear certain types of clothing at certain times it still gave him pretty much the freedom of choice on what to wear. Here are some of the things we came up with:

1. Have him look at the temperature outside. Make a comment as if it is hot, cold, warm or cool. Then make a comment about how he probably might want to dress. Maybe wear

shorts and a T-shirt if it's hot or jeans and a sweatshirt might be better today since it's cold out. Wear your gym shoes and not your sandals since it snowed last night.

2. Something specific they need to wear? Put it out and tell them. "This is what you picked out to wear. I just laid it out for you."

3. Let's say you're going to church or a nicer restaurant. Layout different shirts and slacks. (all that would match) and ask him to pick out what he would like to wear and get dressed and ready. This way you know that no matter what he picks, he will match and he will look nice.

4. Shoes. My father was more comfortable and steady in gym shoes. So we got him a pair in black. This way he could wear the gym shoes with nice pants or suits. Who's going to notice? If you can't find black gym shoes buy the white ones, spray paint them black or even brown, it works perfectly.

Is Your Name Carrot?

There were several restaurants that were favorites of my parents. The food was good, and in the budget, but it was the people that worked there that really made it easy to return to again and again. A little place called Toots was one such place. Mom always knew she could take Dad there and he would eat even if he was having a bad day.

My husband and I joined them quite regularly. The hot dogs were free for kids and our boys loved them, and we loved the chicken tenders, burgers, and cold beer. My mom loved it because it gave her a break and she loved the ribs. The servers were really special and always came around and talked with Dad.

There was one server that, for some reason, Dad always gave a hard time to, teasing her constantly. Her name was Karen. One day he asked her what her name was. To which she replied "Karen." He said, "Carrot?" "No, Karen." She replied. "Oh. I thought you said carrot. I would have to eat you!" She turned, bright red, spun on her heel and walked away. We all died laughing. For some reason that stuck and he always called her carrot. I don't know what it was about Karen or carrot, but he sure had a thing about teasing her.

This shows that it doesn't matter who you are, you can impact the life of someone with Alzheimer's and dementia, or their family. Just being friendly, taking the time to talk to them and never take what is said personally.

Karen was a great sport, and when we saw her years later, at another restaurant, she started laughing about it all over again. Sometimes it takes a village.

No Filters

"You are dumber than a box of rocks!" "B. S.!" Usually followed by the hand signal designating the same thought. These were some of the things that would come out of Dad's mouth. The saying that he didn't engage his brain before he let out the clutch on his mouth is a very true statement. The filters of our brains tend to become nonexistent with Alzheimer's and dementia. Do you think kids say the darnedest things? You haven't heard anything! See it, say it, no processing in between. It just flows. Sometimes it was really funny and he hit the nail on the head other times we had to do some quick thinking.

It's not only things they say, but, also things they see that will prompt the impromptu sayings. There was a point in time when my father was really bothered by the sight of a really obese person. And if we saw them in a restaurant, the comment could go from, "quick order before there isn't any food left." To, "My God! Did you see the size of that person? I bet they needed two chairs!"

It got to the point where we would scope out the restaurant before we walked in to see the lay of the land. We would walk to our table in a different direction or have someone on the opposite side distracting Dad so he wouldn't notice. We also made sure that he would have his back to that particular party when we were seated. He didn't mean anything by it it just came out.

SANDY TOMLIN

About a year after we lost Dad, I had a pretty bad car accident, and a severe concussion. Several years later, I was still opening my mouth only to change feet. I wouldn't realize what I had said, until I saw the shocked look or heard my name called out sternly.

I still cry when I think about those times. Even though, I know I was forgiven, I still feel awful. The one thing I am thankful for is, to my knowledge, Dad never realized that what he was saying was potentially hurtful. He would have been like me, finding it hard to forgive himself for the blunder and hurting people. If there is a grace to this disease that would be it.

Zulu Time

One of the shows on TV that really held my dad's interest was "Jag." He loved the military story line, and whenever they talked about Zulu time, he would look at his watch and let us know exactly what time that was. If they were marching, he would do his own private inspection to make sure the sailors or marines were looking sharp and smart. And he loved it when someone was getting a real dress down (getting yelled at).

When we found out that the show was being discontinued, Mom went out and bought different seasons of "Jag" or we kids would get them for him for his birthday or Father's Day. He was always so happy to get them and to watch them and of course to tell us all about Zulu time every time it came up.

It's great when you can find something that will capture and hold their attention. "Jag" reminded Dad of his Air Force days and those were fond memories.

For those who don't know Zulu time, it is a military name for time which is universal time coordinated or UCT, and Greenwich meantime or GMT. Now, that was just as confusing for me, if not more so. I'm going to try to explain this in an easier way.

It is a geographically fixed time no matter what time zone you may be in. For those in eastern standard time zone you are five hours ahead in UCT so say it is 9 AM, EST. Subtract 5 hours and it is now 0400 Zulu time. So central time it's minus 06:00 and Mountain time is minus 07:00. Note, you will need to use a 24 hour clock not the 12 hour AM PM clock.

By using Zulu time you can coordinate across several time zones and it keeps confusion at bay. Zulu or UCT is also used in navigation. Hope this helps.

Grandma the Great Escape Artist

When we first had to place my grandmother in a nursing facility, she was permitted to go outside. Little did they know she would go for these really long walks. After my mom heard from other families that had family in the facility, that they picked Grandma up a mile away on a very busy road, we were quite concerned. One, that she was up on that road and two, that she got into a car with a total stranger.

A meeting was held, and it was determined that she should have a leg band put on that alarmed every time she went out the door. That didn't stop her. She went anyway. Usually something was always going on that the alarm was not heard or recognized right away, and there she went.

Next there was the code that had to be put in to get the door to open so that she could go out. She was smart enough to stand there and watch in order to figure out the code, put it in and go for her walk. She was a character.

Remember, this all happened years ago, before all this wonderful new technology came about or was even thought of. Grandma was just smart enough to beat the system of that time. Where there's a will there is a way. That nursing facility learned lots of lessons. Thanks to Grandma. What a character she was!

Computer Games

In this day and age of computers, it came in very handy for my family with my dad. Back then, fans could only watch sports o the weekends, Dad enjoyed sports and watching them would keep him entertained and calm.

My boys were into the computer sports games. As it happened one day they were playing on my mom's computer and my dad walked into the room and sat down and started cheering as the computer game was playing. Everyone there had an "ah-ha" moment. Have the boys play their games where Dad can see them and cheer for them; even when the score was as lopsided as 138 to 0. So we moved the monitor out into the great room and the "boys" were happy as can be.

Mom then said, "Now what am I going to do? I don't know how to play these games." So the boys told her how to put the game on auto play so it would play by itself. So, if Mom had things to do, she would put a game on and put it on auto play. Dad would sit in there and scream and shout and yell at the computer and she'd be in the kitchen cleaning up or baking cookies or whatever it was she needed to do while Dad was cheering on a computer game, genius!

The moral of the story is any port in the storm. By sheer luck we were able to capture a pleasure that spans several generations and put it to work for us and our situation. It gave the boys more time with their grandfather, and that in turn gave my mom time to get whatever cleaning or paperwork she needed to get done mostly uninterrupted.

It also made the boys feel important to contribute to Paps' care. You're never too young or old to come up with an inspired idea in any given situation.

We Drove 100 Miles for That?

My mom had five sisters. She was the fourth of the five. They called her Lil Joe Lewis when she was growing up, a famous boxer of the time. So that should give you a major hint as to her personal drive, one that still rings true today.

Family was and is always important and helping them when they are in need is priority number one. When her second oldest sister, Dene, could no longer take care of her home and had lost her husband, the two youngest sisters worked together to help out. My mom would drive out weekly with my dad and during their day there they all would go out for a ride or lunch or something so Aunt Dene could get out of the house for a while.

There was one time they had gone for a drive and had driven pretty far and they passed a drugstore that had incontinent pads that my aunt needed as a two for one deal. Mom being mom, figured let's not waste a trip or an opportunity and pulled in and ran inside to purchase the items. When she came out and got in the car Dad asked her what she had bought. When he found out, he replied, "you mean we drove 100 miles just to buy Dene a bunch of Kotex?"

Aunt Dene laughed and laughed and laughed. She talked about that trip and that comment to anyone who would listen for a very long time.

I love this story because it shows my parents' true spirit. That of service, determination, love, and of course, and always humor. Dad never lost his sense of humor, and he made us laugh all the time. It didn't go away just because he couldn't remember people or places anymore. Deep down, he was still Dad, and he still loved to make us laugh.

The Fountain of Youth

We often took my parents with us for rides and to see the sites. My niece was graduating from high school in South Carolina so we all drove down together. It's about an 11- hour drive from our home to Summerville, South Carolina, including stops along the way. We all took turns riding next to Dad to keep him occupied and so no one person got burnt out.

It was Nathan's turn, and we were going through the mountains when Dad had to go to the bathroom. This is nothing unusual, Dad always had to go to the bathroom. So we passed the "Pee Jar" and towel back to Nathan to give to Dad. Now Dad had performed this act countless times before, but on this occasion he let it rip before everything was set. Well it looked like a fountain going off in the back of the van! Mom was hollering, "Stick it in the jar and cover it up!" Ben and I were laughing so hard we could hardly breathe, Rich is trying to drive and poor Nathan. Poor Nate is scarred for life. Not really, he is staring intently out the window wishing the entire scene would just go away. Between Mom and I we were able to get a handle on the cleanup, and we all laughed and joked about it the rest of the trip. No one but Dad sat in the 'fountain' seat for quite awhile. When we sold that van years later, Nate said he was sad to see the "fountain of youth" van go.

Before my father became extremely incontinent, it wasn't unusual to carry the "Pee Jar" in the car. First off, if we weren't near a rest area or near a restroom when he was out of the car, he would just try to whip it out right there and then. So we had to come up with a way we could get him to either sit in the car, or stand between two open doors to go. Secondly, Dad always thought he had to pee. So if you didn't want to stop every 5 to 10 minutes for him to try to go, the "Pee Jar" was the answer.

Later years Depends was the answer, but even then he still wanted that "Pee Jar"

Back to First Grade

Grandpa Remains Active in Class

Despite husband's illness, couple fills crucial role in young people's lives as volunteers at MECC.

by Tracey Carson
Community contributor

Seven years ago, Benjamin Tomlin was a Mason Early Childhood Center first grader in Dona Mason's class. The MECC teacher and her teaching partner Kim Lovett were working on their annual Mother's Day celebration, but it had started to become overwhelming.

"There was just so much to be done. We didn't want our students to lose instructional time, but we knew how very much our first graders wanted everything to be perfect for their moms." That's where Benjamin's mom, Sandy Tomlin, stepped in and offered that her dad, George Wolf, might be just the guy for the job.

Seven years later, Grandpa George, Grandma Loretta Wolf and Sandy remain faithful volunteers in Mason and Lovett's classes who simply never slow down when it comes to going above and beyond for the students.

"This is the most wonderful family – they treat us like gold. It is absolutely unbelievable what they do for us," said Mason, about the hundreds of hours the family dedicates.

Before school begins, George, who suffers from demenita, is on a mission. Under Loretta's watchful eye, he cleans and sorts every marker, clipboard, whiteboard, binder, and pair of scissors for the 52 students in the classes.

> "They plan their vacations around us. We could never do all of this without their support. Whatever we need, whenever we need it, they deliver."
>
> Kim Lovett, on George and Loretta Wolf

He sharpens countless pencils so that the students are ready to start writing as soon as they step into their new classroom.

Mason Intermediate fourth grader Nate Tomlin, Grandpa George Wolf and Mason Middle School seventh grader Ben Tomlin put the finishing touches on the Mother's Day decorations.
Photo by Tracey Carson

But the work takes on a fever-pace beginning in January as the family gears up for the annual Mother's Day event. They cut out paper flowers and glue special inserts for each child's Mother's Day book. They prepare elaborate flower decorations, and this year even helped grow the grass that fills the ceramic vases students made in art class which will act as center pieces during the memorable event.

"They plan their vacations around us. We could never do all of this without their support," said Lovett. "Whatever we need, whenever we need it, they deliver."

Loretta is a force. She scans Hobby Lobby and Joanne Fabric ads to look for deals on stickers for the students, and she breaks down each task for George. The 82-year old caregiver says that she believes volunteering has slowed the progress of her husband's disease.

"If we didn't have this, he'd sit in a chair all day and get worse and worse. They (Lovett and Mason) are a Godsend. If it wasn't for them, I don't know what we'd do."

The MECC teachers are quick to share that the blessing goes both ways. "We loved having Ben and Nate (Tomlin) in class, and we've been blessed to have this family become such a part of ours," said Mason.

local

SECTION B » TUESDAY, JUNE 18, 2013

George Wolf gets instructions on things to do for the summer from first-grade teacher Kimberle Lovett in her classroom at the Mason Early Childhood Center. THE ENQUIRER/LEIGH TAYLOR

Helping kids also helps 82-year-old

Mason school volunteer is not slowed down by his dementia [Page B3]

COVER STORY

ON THE JOB: Watch 82-year-old George Wolf volunteer at school despite his dementia, at Cincinnati.com.

Dementia doesn't slow Mason school volunteer, 82

MICHAEL D. CLARK
@michaeldclark1

I watch out for the interests of families, students and residents in Butler and Warren county schools. Find me at mclark@enquirer.com or on facebook.com/Michael D. Clark.

MASON — George Wolf's dementia may well have overtaken him by now if he wasn't helping out the kids and teachers at a nearby school.

That's the consensus of those who love Wolf, 82, including the two first-grade teachers he volunteers for each school year and during summer break.

The retired General Electric worker and former U.S. Air Force airman volunteers at Mason Early Childhood Center.

In doing so, he is helping himself.

"It's really a godsend that the teachers let him do this," says George's wife, Loretta, who recently took George to the Warren County school to load up on school supplies he will organize during the summer break.

"Otherwise he would be sitting in a chair all day and more and more of his dementia would take over. By keeping him working he doesn't have time to sit there and realize something is wrong."

Wolf started volunteering seven years ago at the recommendation of his daughter, Sandy Tomlin, whose son was then in Dona Mason's first-grade class. An upcoming classroom Mother's Day celebration was proving overwhelming and she needed extra hands for cutting paper, stuffing envelopes and other repetitive tasks suited for Wolf's skill level.

With Loretta – his wife of 58 years – at his side, George goes about his school activities with an enthusiasm and playful temperament unchanged by his progressive dementia. He doesn't talk much. When he does, it's often a short quip alluding to his condition and work.

"You can tell I'm well broke in," Wolf says with a smile while loading boxes of school supplies into his wife's car.

Wolf works on average a combined 20 hours per week at school and at home on school projects. Teachers especially appreciate Wolf's helping hands in the summer.

"(George and Loretta) take all the summer classroom supplies home. They clean all the scissors, check all the glue sticks and clean up the marker boards. He puts together the homework binders and prepares them for the parents at the beginning of the new school year," Mason says.

Wolf's dementia condition is reflective of the umbrella term that covers a number of degenerative mental aliments – including Alzheimer's disease, the most common cause of dementia. The degenerative disease, which involves vascular or other physical changes in the brain, is often associated with advanced aging. Symptoms include impaired short-term memory, misjudgment, verbal difficulties, declining daily functioning and personality changes.

Dr. Susan Schrimpf Davis specializes in osteopathic and geriatric medicine at the University of Cincinnati College of Medicine. She applauds the Mason teachers, saying the volunteer opportunity can slow Wolf's mental decline.

"The key component is maintaining functionality. Dementia robs people of short-term memories, but they still have lots of old memories," Schrimpf Davis says.

There is also an emotional payoff.

"Everyone can get some emotional satisfaction by keeping active. It feels good for them to help and to continue to feel connected," she says.

Tracey Carson, spokeswoman for Mason Schools, says Wolf and his condition are unique among the hundreds of school volunteers in the district.

"George and Loretta are inspiring," Carson says. "Their thousands of hours volunteering over the years have made such an impact on hundreds of children."

Kim Lovett, whose first-grade classroom is joined with Mason's, says Wolf's volunteering is a "double blessing."

"It works great for us, and it works great for (George and Loretta) as well." ■

George Wolf and his wife, Loretta, right, get instructions on how they can help out for the summer from first-grade teachers Kimberle Lovett, left center, and Dona Mason at the Mason Early Childhood Center. THE ENQUIRER/LEIGH TAYLOR

Holy Day of Obligation

The problem with getting older and having Alzheimer's and dementia Is that other things that go wrong with the body don't take a vacation. One such occasion, my father had a procedure done and someone had to stay with him to make sure he didn't pull anything out, including, but not limited to the stitches. He was most comfortable in his recliner chair, so that is where we had him stay.

I elected to stay up during the night so my mom could get a good nights sleep and care for him during the day. My sister-in-law was to take the next night shift. It was a very difficult night, as I had to hold both of his hands at all times. The discomfort he was going through, and lack of sleep, brought on an interesting dilemma.

Dad had gone back to school. In his mind he needed to get his homework finished. No matter how many times I reassured him that he had completed his homework and I had checked it over. He just wouldn't let it drop. Finally out of exhaustion, lack of sleep, and the grace of God, I hit upon a winner.

I knew that Dad went to Catholic grade school, and on certain days known as Holy Days of Obligation, there was no school, and all the faithful attended mass on that day. So I told him that it was a Holy Day of Obligation, and there wasn't any school. That did the trick for about a minute. Then he wanted to know if Fr. Shari needed another altar server for mass. After several reassurances that his favorite priest had enough altar servers, he slept for several hours.

This one came down to knowing my dad's history. He always told us stories about serving mass for Fr. Shari and of course, my brother, sister and I attended Catholic schools growing up so we knew the routine as well.

Call it what you want; historical knowledge, exhaustion, or Divine Inspiration (my personal favorite) it's what we both needed, to get some sleep that night. Amen?!

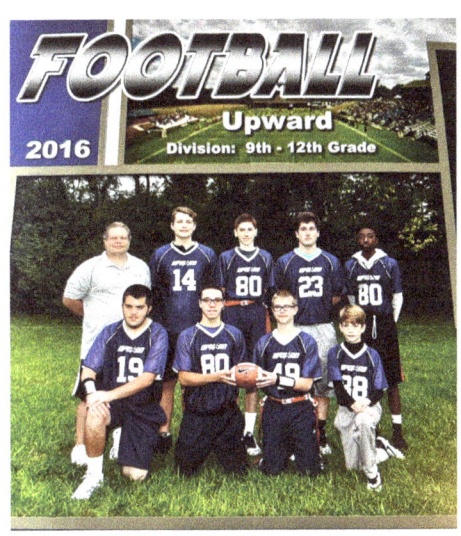

Go! Go! Go!...Wrong Team, Dad

Our boys were very involved in sports from a young age. They started in T-ball and played baseball through college. Second and third grade they tried tackle football and then switch to flag football with Upward. Just a wonderful organization. They played that through eighth grade and even coached for a year or two. They also played basketball with Upward.

My mom and dad rarely missed a game. My dad was always very vocal at our sporting events when we were kids, so I knew what to expect. And like my dad, the apple didn't fall far from the tree when it came to cheering the kids on. With that in mind, the other team members were always informed about my dad, as were any referees and umpires.

You can imagine his confusion when all these kids are running around dressed the same and looking very similar. We would always point out his grandchildren to him, and the number on their jersey and jersey color, but before you know it, Dad is yelling, "Go! Go! Go!" For the other team. We would correct him and tell him again, but it never worked. At least he cheered for both teams equally. Whenever my parents couldn't come everyone wanted to know where my dad was. He was surely loved.

Sandy Tomlin

We never left Dad at home for fear of what he might say or do in public. We wanted him with us, and his grandchildren wanted him there as well. I always made a point of alerting everyone and the game officials so that they were aware.

Only one time did a parent take exception to my dad being present at an event, and quite honestly, I felt sorry for her short sightedness and hardness of heart.

It was always so refreshing to see how welcoming and understanding everyone was. Never once did we have to leave because of Dad, although we did witness some grown adults behaving quite badly at times that were asked to leave. He was considered a joy to be around and people and players alike were happy to have him there, no matter who he cheered for.

Table for One

Our church was having a going away party for one of our priest. He was one of the parish's favorites. Though we were happy for him. We were sad to see him go. Fr. Jamie was very special to our family. He drove an hour to Indiana to the church were my parents were married and performed mass and a ceremony for their 50th wedding anniversary.

As we waited in line to sign the book for him, good friends of ours were waiting with us. Dad always got Beth's name right but he never got Jerry's name right. He always called him, "Gary." Finally, it was our turn to sign the book. As we were up there, I gave the pen to Mom for her to sign. Jerry started heckling us, in a playful manner, about how long we were taking. Mom was engrossed with what she was going to write in the book. My dad didn't do his usual. This time he turned around and held up his middle finger and flipped Jerry off! The look that accompanied that gesture spoke volumes. (His usual was to hold one fist up in front of him. He then acted like he was cranking a window open with the other hand, but instead he lifted his middle finger into the air of the fisted hand.) This gesture left no room for question or intent! Now Jerry thought this was hysterical, of course, Mom didn't see it, but the people next in line did, and they were horrified. After I got Dad to put his quick shot trigger finger away, I quickly explain to them the situation with Dad and apologize for his actions. There were many people around, including all the Parish priest, priest friends of Fr. Jamie and priest from neighboring parishes, that saw what Dad did. Some not so happy, most laughing hysterically. The majority of the people in the parish knew about Dad, and that he had Alzheimer's and dementia. Without realizing it, Dad was making people laugh, providing Divine, albeit comic, relief. Therefore, even though she was fit to be tied, it wasn't as bad as Mom thought it was.

However, Mom was so mad and embarrassed when she found out. Mom wanted to take Dad home right away. But we wouldn't let her, we kept saying it was "Gary" who instigated it. And we would look at Jerry who would just smile and chuckle like he had just seen the best comedy show ever! The rest of us were cracking up as well. I also remember Jerry talking to Fr. Jamie and telling him the story of what happened. Seeing Fr. Jamie's eyes open wide and him saying, "No!" And covering his mouth and bending over with laughter. Oh my, what a site! That really made my night knowing that Dad gave Fr. Jamie a parting gift to remember! I can't think of too many people that can give that shot to "Gary" and get away with it.

It turned out to be a really wonderful evening. Mom was glad she stayed, too. To this day we still talk about the "table for one" incident that "Gary" instigated, and, I would say, is quite proud of, it's probably in his top 10! And we still laugh as hard now as we did then. Divine comic relief, Amen?!

Please know when in public, to be prepared for anything. They don't come with a filter. You never know how they are going to interpret something they see or something someone says and how they will react to it.

We refused to keep Dad home because he might do or say something embarrassing. We wanted him with us. Things didn't happen very often, but when they did, we handled it and moved on. Dad was Dad and we love him for it. Period.

Bring the Dogs

My father, and his brother along with their wives, had to make the unfavorable decision to place my grandmother in a nursing facility. A few years before, when they realize that she could no longer drive, they moved her to a senior, living apartment unit. It became obvious that that would no longer work. This was in the late 1970s and there just wasn't a place specific for Alzheimer's care established at that time.

It was after a hospitalization that the family physician said that our family was out of options and she needed to be admitted to an assisted-living facility. She was moved from the hospital directly to that facility. My mom did her laundry every week and often times my siblings, and I would take the opportunity to pick up the old and drop off the new. It was on one such occasion that my brothers' Irish setter was with us and we asked If we could bring him in. Well, Chester was a star! Grandma loved him and proudly walked with us, holding his leash. So many of the patients and staff, alike, couldn't wait to pet him and or see him do his tricks. To see them smile and perk up when Chester walked by or to see them reach out and pet him just was awe inspiring to me to see. Many of these patients usually just sat there in their wheelchair. Now they were smiling and holding their arms out. It was amazing.

After Chester passed, we were constantly asked, "Where is the dog?" By this time, I had a sheltie named Maddie and several years later another named Sadie. They took Chester's place as normal visitors at the facility and the new one Grandma was transferred to. The dogs loved to be pet and would sit in the laps of many of the patients. I would dress them up for different holidays and they would walk through the hallways with Grandma.

As much as these animals were loved and trained, it is important to know that you cannot just take any pet in to a nursing facility. Usually you need to get papers filled out by your pets' veterinarian, showing that you are all up-to-date on their vaccinations, and that the pet needs to be the correct temperament.

Nowadays, there are therapy dogs that have gone through training to visit the sick and those in facilities. If you think your pet would do good in this wonderful service check out American kennel club (AKC) for more information and resources.

@*#! Dad's Walking

Every once in a while, Dad would get a bee in his bonnet and there was no changing his mind. No matter what tricks we pulled out of the hat, he would not go for them. One particular day, he had decided he wanted to go out to his uncles farm in Saint Leon, Indiana. As a boy, he would ride street cars and buses, and who knows what else to get to that farm. It had just finished raining and he was going, period, end of story!

Mom had no choice except to allow him to go, and she quietly followed behind him. He walked all around their neighborhood, and then he cut down behind the lakes and walked the new subdivision behind where they lived. He was walking by one of the small lakes, all wet and muddy, when his legs finally gave out.

Mom went to him. She just had him sit and rest for a bit, he still couldn't get up. A neighbor saw her and came out and helped get him up to a brick wall to sit on. The walk back to their home was too long for him so Mom pulled out her phone and called me. I headed up and pick them both up. Helped her clean him up and we all had a nice cold drink and sat and talked about his good time at Uncle Shorty's farm.

Like I wrote earlier, there are times when people with Alzheimer's dementia get something in their minds and you just cannot change it. There are several ways people choose to tackle this problem. Not all have the means my mom had to follow him. My suggestion is to talk with your caregiver and the support of the village you have to help you care for your loved one. Together figure out your best way to tackle a situation like this. Be prepared for this contingency before it happens. Knowing what to do before hand makes life much easier in the long run.

We wanted Dad with us and not on a drug that would make him sleep. We found a psychologist that not only would help with dad, but help by listening to Mom and helping her as well. We figured out as a team, the best course of action for Dad and his well-being.

I Need a Bag Man

Some days my mom just needed a break. You could hear it in her voice if you called or see it in her face if you were with her. On those days, if I was able, I would go over and pick Dad up. I'd go in and tell Dad that I needed a bag man. That was his cue to carry my bags to the car when we went shopping. It was a chore that he took great delight and pride in doing.

We'd go to different stores and I would always have him push the cart around. He would walk tall and push that cart. It was not the time to browse because he would wait only until something caught his attention. And NO ONE was a stranger. He would talk to anyone whether they knew what he was talking about or not. He would proclaim to everyone that he was my bag man. "She fills them and I carry them." He would have to leave them with a salute and literally march on. Making a comment about not working too hard.

Shopping isn't the only time I took my dad one on one. If I had doctors appointments or dentist appointments he would go with me to those as well. I also took him when I went to vote. Or we would just go to my home to spend time, maybe I'd find some work for him to do at home like dust, swifter the floor, he was great at wringing out rags and handing them to me when I was washing down walls too, things of this nature. Also, we did the reverse, I would keep Dad at my parent's house, and Mom would take off and spend some time shopping or doing whatever it was that she needed to do. Anything to give Mom some time to herself.

However, usually Dad got more upset if Mom left the house. He would worry about her. If we left the house, he didn't worry about her. He was more concerned about doing his job as the bag man. Be cognizant of what causes more anxiety and strive to avoid those situations.

It's important to make sure the main caregiver gets breaks to be by themselves. Mental and physical health is just as important for them as it is for the person who has Alzheimer's and dementia. Even if it's to let them clean the house uninterrupted. Or just to sit and be is sometimes all that is needed. To recharge the batteries, so to speak.

It takes a village, but the mayor of the village needs the help of the assistants. If you look at it in another way, it's great one on one time you get to spend with your loved one. Precious moments that will be such beautiful memories in the future to recall. Some of my most favorite times are times I had my dad one-on-one. We had a blast together! I miss his spontaneous,

"I love you, San."

"I love you, too, Dad."

Dad and Kathy Sitting on a Swing

Through the law of averages, we all got hit with something we would rather not have. This time it was my mom's turn. she was in the hospital and had to have surgery. Usually, when or if mom is hospitalized, Dad just stayed in her room during the day with her and one of us would take him home and spend the night with him and bring him back the next day. He was content, Mom was his lifeline and he sat in the chair next to her bed.

However, this was going to be a lengthy surgery so my sister-in-law stayed at home with Dad while my brother and I sat in the waiting room. While she was home with Dad, Kathy decided to take him out on the deck and sit in the glider with him. It wasn't long and Dad reached over and held her hand. Kathy didn't think anything of it. As they went to get up to go in, my dad quickly leaned in and stole a kiss. Kissing her full on the lips! Poor Kathy! He said he wanted to give her a kiss before they went inside. She kept her distance, not wanting to give him the wrong impression or encourage him.

Later, during the same hospitalization, Tom and Kathy took Dad out to their place in Indiana to stay for a few days. The one evening Dad asked Kathy if he was bunking with her. They got that straightened out and Tom told Kathy to give him (Tom) a kiss good night and go in the master bedroom and lock the door. He would get Dad settled in the other bedroom and he would sleep on the couch to keep an eye on things.

One thing that we found out about Alzheimer's and dementia, also, TIAs (small strokes), depending on where they are in the brain, it can block those areas that inhibit such things. They can cause a change in language, causing someone who may never cuss to start cussing or using vulgar, suggestive language. Sometimes sexual advances like a kiss or a pinch may occur. I often wondered if Kathy looked like an old friend of Dad's maybe that's what caused him to do that, maybe it was something in his brain or lack there of that caused him to do that. At any rate, things that people would never do or even think of doing or saying before, they are now doing and sometimes with regularity. Dad would never have asked Kathy for a kiss, much less stole a kiss from her in such a manor. He was a man of honor and it just wasn't in his make up before Alzheimer's and dementia. Again, it is something we can look back on and laugh. But at the time, it had to be alarming to Kathy. She handled herself, my dad and the situation with grace and beauty.

Lost and Found

Twist, pull, blow, drop, repeat. A lot of those afflicted with Alzheimer's and dementia, are fiddlers. They fiddle with anything and everything. The main things for my dad were his hearing aids, his wedding ring, and his watch. I can't begin to count the number of times he would take his hearing aids out, blow them out, turn them on and off and put them back in. His wedding ring, he would spin on his finger constantly. And his watch, we had to reset on almost a daily basis.

Dad had lost some weight, so his ring was loose on his finger. Mom noticed one day that his ring of 63 years was gone. She was devastated. She tore the house apart looking for it and came up with nothing. She went out and bought a cheap one for him to wear, because he was missing it, too. About three days later she was vacuuming, and there it was in the middle of the floor! She thought it was the cheapy that she got him and he had lost it, but no, it was the original. To this day, we don't know where it came from.

As Catholics, we always say a prayer to Saint Anthony when we are trying to find something. Asking for his intercession and help in finding the item. Of course, we were all saying that prayer and asking for his help when Dad lost his wedding ring and Mom was trying to find it. Could it be? Maybe. We don't know but, we believe it was. Thank you, Saint Anthony, because it sure made my mom awfully happy to have found the original wedding band. She picked it up and put it away. This way she knew she had it so when Dad passed, he could be buried with his wedding ring.

Moral of this story, any jewelry, which has any value, monetary or personal, find replacements for them. Don't wear the original wear a cheap imitation instead. We did this for my grandmother at the nursing facility as well, we didn't want her to lose her rings either. They could have fallen off, come off with her clothing when she changed, could have been 'borrowed' by other patients, or just been taken.

This goes for any type of jewelry, bracelets, rings, earrings, necklaces, and broaches. Better to get a cheap piece of costume jewelry, than to be heartbroken over the loss of a family heirloom. Another thing is to take pictures so if a piece is lost, you can show it and hopefully, match it up with lost and found items.

Other items that you want to make sure your loved ones don't carry around either in their wallet, or in their purses: drivers license, Social Security cards, insurance cards, credit cards, anything like this that has their information on it that could be stolen or taken and copied down. If they like carrying car keys, give them an obsolete key on a key chain to carry in their pocket. They are very vulnerable at this stage, very trusting. Although it is of utmost importance to treat them with dignity, and not as a child, you have to be vigilant as if they were a child.

The New Hat

One of the unfortunate things of growing older are the injuries from falling. Add to that the confusion of Alzheimer's and dementia, and you have quickly compounded the issue. While in the care of the nursing facility, my grandmother fell and split her head. This is life, it happens. The nurse could have been standing right next to her and it still could happen. Per protocol, she was taken to the emergency room and my parents were called. I happen to be home when my mom got the call, so I went along with her to the hospital.

When we arrived and inquired about her, they replied that she was being very combative, and not leaving her bandage in place. They were going to have to restrain her. Mom and I knew if we could get back there with her we could hopefully keep that from happening. The nurse was very understanding and allowed us back with her and Grandma was having a tizzy fit.

She kept saying she wanted that thing off her head. She didn't like it. When I looked at her, I realize that her head was bandaged in such a way that it resembled a hat. Now my grandmother was always a fashionable lady so I told her that I liked her new hat. She stopped and said, "my new hat?" "Yeah, it's really cute." I opened up the tray so she could see the mirror. She looked in the mirror. She looked this way, and that way, and then pronounced, "it is cute, but I think it needs a pin." We all laughed, she settle down and things went much better.

Things have changed a lot since the early 1980s. Families with Alzheimer's and dementia usually go right on in with their loved ones DEPENDING ON THE SITUATION. Each situation is different and you should always defer to the experts of the medical professionals as to if you are able to be with your loved one. Don't take it personal if it's not possible. It's just that they can't get you back there at that time or they don't want you back there at that time because of procedures that they have to perform.

They want your help to keep your loved ones calm, but circumstances dictate what can or cannot happen. Be sure and let them know anything specific that may help in the case of the individual. This may be of great help to them to keep them calm while you are not able to be with them. Work together with the medical professionals. They will appreciate it, your loved one will benefit from it and you will feel better about it. It makes for a great team effort and gives your loved ones the best care possible.

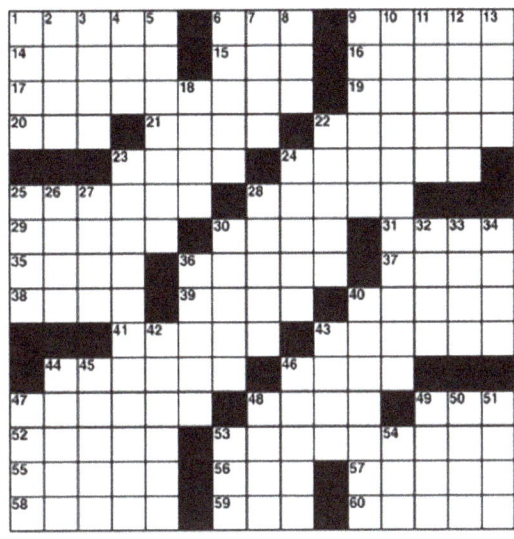

Crossword Anyone?

It's always a challenge when any loved one enters the hospital, but if that loved one has Alzheimer's and dementia, it can really be a challenge. For us, one of the challenges was making sure my mom took care of herself while Dad was in the hospital. So my siblings and I, often times the grandchildren as well, stayed with Dad during the day, so Mom could be with him during the evenings and nights. On one such occasion, Dad was scheduled for an MRI. Now how in the world were we going to get him to hold still? First thing first, it was my day to be there with him and I was told there was a back up in the x-ray department. They would keep him in the room as long as possible, but he may have to wait once he was down there. Oh boy!

Thankfully, Mom had left the paper behind. When it was time to go, I grabbed the comic section and took it with us. Usually, giving Dad the comics to read worked, but the wait was too long. So I started asking him to help me with the crossword puzzle. I looked for clues I thought he would be able to solve, and he was knocking them out. We had solved several of the riddles by the time it was his turn to go in.

After explaining to the technician that I most probably could keep him calm during the test, he was more than happy to have me as a partner. They allowed me to go in as they got Dad strapped down, and I talk to him and explained why that was happening. I assured him I would be in the next room the whole time. Of course, I couldn't stay in there because of the magnetism, but they did, however; allow me in the observation room with the microphone. The tech would explain what was going on and what was going to happen, and if Dad had any strange questions, they looked at me and I was able to explain it in a way that made sense to Dad..

The test went smoothly and the tech thanked me for my assistance, but I really thanked him for allowing me to be with Dad in such a way that it all worked out. I was really blessed, I had never heard of this happening before. I don't know if this is common practice or if the tech just recognize that we could help each other. Either way, I was very thankful.

No Touchy

My dad had a very hard touch. He was the one who always snapped things off because he had to tighten it just one more twist. His side of the closet or cabinets were always worn down because he just had to smack it closed with one good shove. His handshakes were no different. He taught all three of us to have a firm handshake and to look the person in the eye. There is nothing worse, in his eyes, then to shake a "dead fish" during a handshake. As he would say, "no limp dicks!" Of course, we were much older before he chose that form of verbiage.

His handshake was like putting your hand in a vice and having it tighten to the point that you were in pain. As his Alzheimer's and dementia progressed, my mom had to be very vigilant of who he was near. If it was an elderly person, they definitely were off limits to his Herculean shake. She didn't want him to hurt anyone by accident. She would grab his right hand and tell him, "no, don't touch anyone. You don't want to hurt anyone." He would say, "Aw, Mom (he always called her Mom.) I won't hurt anyone" And she was quick to reply, "no, you won't mean to, but it could happen."

It is amazing the strength of older people. If that person is unaware of the power behind their grip or punch it certainly can do some damage. Especially to another elderly person or someone who is caught off guard.

It's not that they are mean, that is not the intent. It is just a compulsion that overtakes them sort of like a flight or fight instinct. My mom knew my dad would try to shake everyone's hand he came across. The easiest thing to do was to hold his right hand. That way he wouldn't shake hands. Therefore, there was no touchy!

Keep Him Busy

No one slept during the day in Mom's house, at least, not until all your work was finished. Mom is a country, girl, born and raised. She is one of the smartest people I know. Her ability to figure out how to organize, work smarter, not harder, fix it if it's broken, and if it's worth doing it is worth doing right the first time, are all wonderful lessons that she taught all of us. So it should come as no surprise to those who know her that she came up with a way, in our opinion, to keep Dad from getting worse. She did this by keeping him mobile, busy and using his brain. She was doing everything to slow the progress down.

You've already read about the years Dad spent helping Kim and Dona, the first grade teachers. Here are some of the other things we did:

House cleaning. Dad always ran the vacuum cleaner. When it was time for spring cleaning, he went from being our bag man to our rag man. He would wring out our rags and hand them to us as we washed down walls or cleaned windows. He also was great at doing the rug shampooer or should I say holding the cord for us, so it wouldn't get in our way. Cleaning screens with the hose, rinsing the plates and loading and unloading the dishwasher just to name a few.

Canning and freezing. We make our own applesauce and we would get bushels of apples. I have an apple peeler slicer. We had a system. I put the apple on, Dad cranked to peel and slice the apple, I took the finished apple off and put it in lemon water. Mom went through them from there. After we had added all the ingredients and blended them to the consistency of our liking Dad would hold the bags while I filled them, and then Mom would label them and in the freezer they went. Next we would do corn pretty much the same way. Tom usually joined us for the shucking party (pulling the corn husks and silk off). Then we would cut the corn off the cob. Cook it and add the ingredients and the bagging process would take place once again.

Quilting. In the winter, Mom set up a quilting frame and she went and purchased fleece material. She would pin two layers together and draw lines with material marking pencils on the fleece. She would then sit Dad down in front of it, and he would hand stitch along those lines and make quilts. I bet he made at least 50 or more and they were all donated to the homeless shelter in Cincinnati. He also made one for each grandchild for Christmas presents. I can tell you those are cherished and the favorite blanket of all of them. One is displayed in the picture for this chapter. If you look closely, you can see his stitching in white thread.

Sewing. My mom and I love to sew and there's nothing we like better than sewing together. So when we sew, after we cut things out and get the initial pinning done, I usually sew and she presses and pins the next step. With Dad, we sat him next to me and he was my pin puller. He would pull the pins from the material as it came from the back of the sewing machine. Sometimes he would get ahead of me and I might have to re-pin things, but that was OK. I miss my pin puller when I sew now.

So you see the possibilities are endless of how you can have your loved one help you and keep them busy. It can be as easy as having them help fold laundry, to helping them cook. When we made Christmas cookies, Dad was the scooper. He would scoop all of the cookie dough and we would put them in the freezer. Then when the kids came over, we would pop them in the oven and we'd have cookies and we would decorate the sugar cookies with Nana, which is a yearly tradition. As you can see, by doing this you are helping them. And more often than not, they are helping you. Sometimes it takes your patience and sometimes you have to redo things, but in the end, it's totally worth it.

Charleston Chew

On one of their trips to Cincinnati, my cousin, Gary and family found out one of my father's favorite candy was French Chew. But then, after a visit to my sister's, he got hooked on Charleston Chew. After going home, Gary did some research and found out that Charleston Chew is made by Tootsie Roll Industries. He dug a little deeper and found out where he could purchase this candy.

On March 13th, Dad's birthday, a package arrived in the mail. Low and behold it was a box filled with Charleston Chew for Dad. Mom had to take the box and hide it because he would have eaten all of them in a single sitting. She would give him a few every day until they were gone. Every year on his birthday and at Christmas, a package would arrive for Dad, and it would be filled with Charleston Chew.

Simple acts of kindness. It's just so nice, and it means so much. It made my dad's day every time he got to eat one of those Chews. Something so so easy yet, such a wonderful treat.

If you think, oh, that is so little; it won't mean anything; they won't know who sent it.

Wrong! Wrong! And maybe.

It doesn't matter how little the gesture, if it has a connection to their past or something they like it will be a hit. It will mean something! It will make them smile, and that is always worth the time and effort to do something nice for someone. Yeah, they may not know who sent it, but so what. Just doing it will do your heart good!

Let's Go Look at Christmas Lights

"This is where I live! I am not leaving!" Oh boy, here we go again. We always brought Grandma home as much as possible. For dinner or to sit out on the back patio, things of that nature. Especially during the holidays we always had her there to watch the great grandkids open their gifts or watch us decorate. As Grandma got older, it sometimes became a task to get her back out the front door to go back home to the nursing facility. In fact, one time she nearly pushed Mom off the front steps. So we had to get creative when it was time to go home.

Sometimes someone else would take her home and tell her they wanted to take her for a ride in their car. But the one thing that always worked the best during the holidays was driving around, looking at all the Christmas lights. She loved them! We would put on Christmas music and take the back roads all the way back. We would cut down side streets if we saw something really pretty, anything to make it last longer and make it really special for her. She would oooo! And aaah! And point things out that she thought were really beautiful and we would agree with her and we would find things that we thought were really neat and point those out to her. We would sing Christmas carols together on key or off key, it didn't matter. We just had a wonderful time being with her and taking that ride looking at the Christmas lights.

Here are some items you may find helpful. If an Alzheimer's and dementia, patient doesn't want to do something, be prepared they can be just as stubborn and as strong as a mule. And yes, they do kick and bite at times. Handle with care!

When they are feeling insecure, they may asked to go home. It may be that it is too noisy or too many people around it could be overwhelming for them. But if they are comfortable and happy, and you need to get them back, you best have some tricks up your sleeves or they aren't going to budge.

Golden Anniversary

On October 1, 2005, my parents celebrated their golden anniversary. They would be blessed to celebrate 13 more years together before my father passed. We had been dealing with my dad's Alzheimer's and dementia for more than 10 years at this point.

My sister, brother and I had a party for Mom and Dad, starting with a Catholic mass and renewal of their wedding vows at the very church they were married in 50 years ago. The priest from our present parish, Fr. Jamie Weber, drove over an hour to perform the service. The two granddaughters that played instruments played along with another family friend who played the trumpet and the organist. Another family friend sang.

It was a beautiful mass that we all participated in. But before they walked down the aisle, Dad asked Fr. Jamie not to talk too long. Fr. Jamie relayed this and he said he didn't know how to cut 50 years together short. My parents were married for 63 years almost 64. No matter how bad his days got, their love never failed. He always knew he loved Mom even if he didn't always know her.

Thankfully, the day of their golden anniversary Dad was in good shape, and we all had a blast, as did our guests. We had everyone that was in their wedding party present, except for one. And we all had a wonderful time celebrating their love. My brother, sister, and I counted our blessings at having such wonderful parents, and being part of such a loving family.

It was there that we saw the cousins on my grandmother side of the family. A large number of them stricken with the same ailment, but some of them much worse than Dad. After seeing this, we were doubly thankful for God's blessings. Afterwards, some people came up and said they expected Dad to be worse. "Why he seems fine!" Was the comment. Please keep in mind that you are just seeing a snapshot of that person. You have no idea what it is like to live with or care for them 24/7. Until you have walked a mile in their shoes, and at this point, I don't know whether it would be a good or bad thing. Don't make those assumptions. Because you just don't know what you don't know.

Pee on the Plane

Our family always traveled. Dad would plan where we would go and we would pack up the old '63 station wagon with no air conditioning and head out on our next adventure. We never did the same thing twice and visited many states and saw many wonders. One of the most memorable was when the American Falls of the Niagara Falls was turned off. Now that was a sight! We could pitch the tent or take it down in under five minutes.

Later years, they got an RV and the four older grandchildren really had fun with Nana and Papa in his big truck. Mom and Dad traveled out west and many other places with my Uncle Bill and Aunt Kathy.

Unfortunately, this had to come to an end as Alzheimer's and dementia raised its ugly head. Mom couldn't drive 11 hours to visit my sister with Dad so they had to fly. When someone went with them, she didn't have to worry about bathroom breaks, but when she was by herself, it was a race to get to the rest room. They didn't have family restrooms yet. So if she had to go, she had to make sure he stayed put, worrying the entire time she was in the ladies room, and then as quickly as possible get out and get him. Then she had to get him to the mens room. Hope he didn't take too long and then get to the plane on time. If they had a connecting flight this often presented a huge problem because Dad always needed to use the bathroom. Or thought he did if he saw one.

So what did Mom do? She made sure they used the lavatory on the plane once they took off and before they landed. Once again, communication was key. The flight attendants were aware of what she needed and usually assisted her if needed.

This way she was able to get him through the airports without fear of missing flights or of having him wander off on her or if she needed to use the bathroom. He couldn't go anywhere on the plane. And the flight attendants were right there to tell him where Mom was if he got worried or missed her. What a novel idea.

The Night Before Christmas

Mom always comes up the greatest ideas for Christmas. One year she decided that she was going to get the record a book for all of us kids for Christmas so she got the book *The Night Before Christmas* and she and Dad sat in the other room and read the books and recorded them for us. I happen to be at their house at the time that they were doing this. When they were finished, Dad came out and he sat down next to me and he said, "San, do you want me to tell you the story *The Night before Christmas*?"

I said, "Sure Dad." And I thought to myself, "oh, this oughta be good."

So as I sat there on the couch next to my dad and listen to his rendition of *The Night before Christmas*, I found myself laughing so hard I had tears coming down my cheeks. I then began to howl because I was laughing so hard, next I actually fell off the couch laughing! I was holding my stomach and my sides because they hurt so badly from laughing so hard. I had never heard the story told this way before.

Mom came out and asked what all the commotion was. I explain to her what I had just heard, still wiping tears from my eyes.

"Oh yes. That's the one he learned when he was in the Air Force." She said. "You kids have never heard that before?"

"No! I'm in my 40's and I have never heard that before," I replied.

I then asked my brother and my sister if they had ever heard it before, they agreed with me, they had never heard it before either. So I got him to say it again and I taped it. I played it for the rest of the family, except my two young sons, and I got the same reaction from them that Dad got from me. We laughed so hard we all cried.

My youngest, Nathan, always the curious one, wanted to hear this story so every time he got Paps alone, he would say, "Tell me the story of *The Night before Christmas,* Paps." Dad would get started and I would say, "No! No! You can't say that to him!" This went on for years, Nathan trying to get Dad to tell him the story. We found out after Dad had passed that he was successful on at least one occasion. It has now become a family tradition to play the recording of Dad saying his rendition every Christmas Eve after we're finished opening the presents.

This rendition has made its rounds with friends and family alike. We always laugh that he couldn't remember his wife of 63 years. He couldn't remember that he had peed just five minutes ago, but he could remember this, priceless!

Authors note: I am now going to write out my father's rendition of *The Night before Christmas*.

Please note, it is not for everyone. It definitely is not for younger children, nor people who would find vulgarity and slang offensive, so please read at your own risk.

"Twas the night before Christmas and all through the house.

The whole damn family was drunk as a louse.

With Maw at the cat house and Paw out of jail,

I crawled in bed for a good piece of tail.

Grandma and Grandpa were singing a song,

The kids upstairs were flogging their dongs.

When out on the lawn I heard such a clatter,

I sprang from my wife to see what was the matter.

Away to the window I flew like a flash,

I tore open the shutter and fell on my ass.

By the crest of the moon on the new fallen snow,

Gave whore house luster to objects below.

There to my bloodshot eyes did appear,

A little ole sleigh with two mangy reindeer.

A little ole drunkard with his hand on his dick,

Yeah, I knew that must be St. Nick.

Slower than snails his reindeer they came,

He cursed and he bitched and he called them by name.

Now Dicker, now Pricker, step on those walls,

Hurry goddamn you, I'll cut off your balls.

He staggered and stumbled on down towards the door,

He tripped on his dong and fell on the floor.

I heard him exclaim as he rose out of site,

Piss on you all, it's a hell of a night!

                                  Merry Christmas!

Tootsie

My father loved dogs. As his condition increased in severity we noticed that the dogs in our family never shied away from him and they were soothing for him as well. Mom and Dad were in their late 70s early 80s respectively and Mom could see how the dogs helped, so she made the decision to get a dog for Dad.

At first we were going to get one that was older and trained, but then I started doing some research. For our situation it seemed that a puppy would be the better answer. The reasons were so that the dog will grow and learn Dad's ways and be comfortable with that. Of course, the family would always be around to make sure all went well. Or be ready to step in quickly if needed. Also, it was important that Dad name the dog. This way it would be easier for him to remember the name. The dog would not be a babysitter, but definitely there to help keep him calm.

We found a little gem at a rescue farm and drove several hours to get her. She was tiny and didn't mind being held. Dad started calling her Toots. He would hold her and talk to her, and it always started with, "Hey Toots!" From that we named her Tootsie. He took her everywhere, to stores, church, restaurants, even airplanes to visit my sister in South Carolina. She was welcomed as part of the family, especially at our church. She was the fourth dog that performed a service to join our parish family.

Tootsie would sit with Dad and he would turn her head to look out the window, or watch TV with him. She sat on the glider with him, something she continues to do even though he is gone. And she was always there for him to love on pet and play with. Now that Dad is gone, Tootsie performs another service. She keeps Mom on her toes, if that's possible. She gets up in the chair with Mom just like she did with Dad. Mom talks to her and cares for her and enjoys the connection the two of them share. She goes everywhere with Mom, even on the plane to South Carolina. She doesn't go to the stores or anything, but she does follow Mom around quite a bit. And when she piddles where Dad missed the toilet quite often, (even though Mom has scrubbed and scrubbed and scrubbed) she gets Mom's full attention, wanted or not. "You damn dog!"and we all laugh and say, "you know you love her."

The decision to get a puppy, or a dog at any age or of any type is not something that should be done on a whim. Careful thought, and consideration should be given to the cost, care and responsibility of this pet. It takes time and effort, especially at first. It is an added burden for the caregiver until the dog is trained and comfortable. A care plan definitely needs to be put into place to help the main caregiver during this period. My sister came in from South Carolina and stayed with my parents to help my mom train Tootsie and care for my dad. My brother and I and our families also pitched in. We are so blessed to be able to have each other to count on and to know that each other will be there if needed.

SANDY TOMLIN

Thank God for Comics

When Mom had a doctor appointment she usually took Dad with her. Unfortunately, when it comes to a mammogram you can't do that quite so easily. My sister-in-law, Kathy, was available and went along with them to this appointment. Mom gave Kathy the comics from the paper and told her every time he got antsy to just give him the paper to read and it will settle him down.

Sure enough, Mom gets called back and Dad sits there for a bit then starts peppering Kathy with questions about where Mom went, is she OK, no really what is wrong with her, etc. As instructed, out came the comics and Dad would read them. He would point out the ones he thought were funny to her. He loved Dennis the Menace, Hi and Lois, BC and Snuffy Smith. During an approximately 45 minute wait she estimated that he read them maybe 15 different times. Each time he pointed out the exact same comics that he thought were funny.

It's funny the look, you get from people as you're sitting there with someone who has Alzheimer's and dementia. They range from horror and sadness to smiles, and sometimes tears. Other times they are glued to your every word and action with your loved one. Often and not unusual, people would come up and ask us about Dad, and how wonderful it is, that we take him out. Or they may ask our advice on something. This at first amazed us, but then we kind of got used to it. I never would consider leaving Dad behind and we treated him how we always did. We treated him with love and respect.

GPS Directions

Turn left here. In 600 feet take the second turn on the roundabout. Recalculating! Oh, we did something wrong and the GPS we nicknamed Maude is not happy.

While on our trip in Germany with Mom and Dad, the rental car was equipped with GPS. This made it very convenient for me to drive them around while Rich worked during the day. It came in quite handy, but on the day we left to come home, had we known, we could have put it to use in a much more practical way.

We were on our way to the airport, when my father had to use the men's room. (Something new and different.) We pulled into a gas station so he could go. We waited and we waited and we waited some more. Rich went in to check on him, but he said he was fine and still in the stall. After another 10 to 15 minutes of waiting, Rich was getting antsy that we were going to be late getting to the airport. So my mom went in then and got him out. Come to find out he didn't even go! He was just sitting there waiting to go.

So we start the car up and the GPS talks to Rich and tells him which way to go.

My dad says, "Hey, that's pretty slick! She just talks and tells you what to do."

Rich answers, "Well, if we had known that Dad, we would have piped her into the bathroom and told you to wipe your ass, pull up your pants, wash your hands and get a move on!"

I didn't think my dad was ever going to stop laughing at that one.

There are times when the bathroom becomes an obsession often times Alzheimer's and dementia patients will sit for long periods of time, or they will think they have to go every five minutes or forget that they just went to the bathroom or they may be doing some artwork you would really rather not deal with in there. All of the above for Dad.

It is what it is. One note to be watchful for is a urinary track infection as it can make the condition and confusion worse. If an older senior becomes confused, that is usually one of the first things they check for. Make sure they stay well hydrated. Make sure with keeping them hydrated that you do not give them caffeinated drinks because that will just make them more dehydrated, no soft drinks, tea, coffee, things of that nature or at least cut back as much as possible on them. It may mean more trips to the bathroom, ugh, but it beats the alternative.

Did You Have Enough Rubbers?

On another visit to Cincinnati, my cousin, Gary and his family had recently visited Disney World in Florida. While they were regaling us with their stories and adventures, Gary mentioned that he had run into a guy he worked with and his family. As it so happened, this gentleman and his family had to leave early and they still had three days left of their planned and paid for vacation. Rather than let the room sit empty, he offered it to Gary, Gloria and kids when they discovered that they would be leaving at the same time.

So Gary was telling my dad how, when they first arrived they stayed at one resort, and a few days later switched to another one. Then because of his friends gracious offer they switched rooms yet again for the rest of their stay. My dad looked at Gary and asked him if he had packed enough rubbers. Gary said he he didn't understand what my dad meant. My dad said, "Rubbers! You know for all that bed hopping you were doing."

How funny that Gary didn't get that Dad was referring to condoms in the old slang of the 50s. Had Gary given it just a thought, he would have been right there with Dad and would have laughed right along side of Dad. But instead, the joke was on him.

The old sense of humor was the old time sense of humor, and Gary needed to travel back to be there with my dad to see it. Gary still tells the story and laughs about how he didn't pick up on it, and how my dad gave him a hard time for not knowing what a rubber was.

Loved that Silky Feel

Where is my Blankey? I have to have my pillow! There are so many people these days that have to have certain things a certain way. Well, the same can be said for those with Alzheimer's and dementia. My grandmother loved that silky feeling, she would sit there with a blanket that had the silk like binding on it, and she would just rub it between her fingers to the point that it would wear out and Mom would have to be replace it. But it kept her calm, so it was worth the effort, time and trouble that it took. My grandmother, loved that silky feeling on anything, her clothes, her pajamas, her pillowcases, you name it she loved it.

When Grandma would visit we would always make sure that we had something near that she could hold, whether it was a pillow, a blanket, something like that that was soft and silky that she could pet or rub between her fingers anything like that that would keep her calm, and that she would like. If we went out to eat, it was always a tissue or napkin that she held in her hand.

Now, my dad was a horse of a different color. His thing was he liked things tight. Big surprise there! Sometimes he would come out with his belt so tight we wondered how in the world he was able to breathe.

Mom would say, "Dad you need to loosen your belt up!"

His usual reply was, "then my pants will fall down."

His shoes were the same way. He tried them so tight that he would have marks on his feet afterwards even though he had thick socks on. If the boys would ask him to tie their shoes, we always would say, "Loosely! Loosely!" because he would make them so tight.

He also had to swing his keys around on his finger. So that he wouldn't lose the car keys. Mom got some old obsolete keys and put them on a key ring, and gave them to him to carry. That was all he needed. Oh yeah, it had to have a nail clipper on it, too. He constantly was trimming his fingernails. That nail clipper came in handy because sometimes we needed to borrow it.

The thing is both Dad and Grandma were comfortable with these items being the way they were. And if that helped them feel good, feel calm, feel better about themselves, then that was a good thing. But with Dad we did have to make sure he wasn't having things too tight and cutting off his circulation.

Is My Mom Dead?

As dementia progresses, the patient slides back into the past more and more and short-term memory becomes less and less. My father was at an era in his life, where he realized his parents, most importantly, his mother, who was not around. He got into a cycle where he was constantly asking if his mother was dead.

My mom would explain that she was. She reassured Dad he was right by her side and how he asked her to hang on an hour until it was Mother's Day. As it happened, she did stay with us until Mother's Day. My dad and grandmother were 69 and 91 years old, respectively at the time of her death.

It's hard to answer the same question over and over again. At one time, we came into their home and saw a note taped to the trusty lampshade. On the note, it read "yes, your mother is dead. Yes, you were with her when she passed and at her funeral." While it is hard to constantly answer the same questions over and over again, it's worse to see them relive the pain of loss each time they realize their loss, and that they have no recall of it.

My mom actually had a copy of her obituary laminated and placed it in Dad's wallet. Whenever he wanted to go down that road, she would tell him to look in his wallet. He would find the obituary, read it out loud and quietly put it back in his wallet. Sometimes he would ask different questions about it, other times he would just sit there quietly. And it may or may not start again. But it is seemed to ease the hurt of seeing the pain he would go through.

To me that's the hardest thing to witness. When they become aware that they have an issue and they have lost out on time. Or when they realize that they have lost a loved one and they don't remember. They feel that pain all over again, it's so hard to see the look of hurt in their faces. It makes you want to cry but you can't, you have to acknowledge the pain that they are feeling and reassure them that yes, they were there and they felt that pain then and you were there with them as well, but then you've got to pull them out of it and get them to move on to something else.

Hi, Dad

⚜

Grandpa Wolf, he is one for the books. He was a jack of all trades and master of a few. He was a semiprofessional football player. He was a bar owner and bartender, Ice man and a fireman. Those are the ones that I can remember there may be more I'm sure there was. I remember a story where he put Dad on his stomach, and he swam on his back across the Ohio River when Dad was a child. He was a short, stocky, tough, strong man. And as kids, we never wanted to find out if his bark was worse than his bite. If they handed out awards for being a good father or husband, unfortunately Grandpa would not have won any.

As Dad got older and his Alzheimer's and dementia progressed more and more stories came out about he and his father, many not so happy. Grandpa wasn't all bad, he could be really great if he wanted to. He was an avid reader, he could do The New York Times crossword puzzles with a pen. And what all of the grandkids marveled at was he had all of his teeth removed, but he never wore his dentures and he could eat steak with just his gums. No kidding!

So is it any wonder that whenever Rich would come in my parents' home and my dad would say, "Hi Dad." it would ruffle Rich's feathers. Rich is tall, strong and stocky. Both he and my grandfather had gray hair, both combed their hair, straight back and both wore glasses.

Those were the only similarities. But for Dad it was enough for him to get it in his head that Rich was his father. If Grandpa had a better reputation with the family, I don't think Rich would have minded so much Dad calling him that, but of course the fact was that Grandpa mistreated Dad and Grandma. My husband did not want to be associated with that type of character at all. Of course it didn't help when my mom and I said, "well yeah, I guess we can see the similarity." that just made Rich madder.

This went on for quite a while, well over a year. Every time Dad would say

"Hello Dad" to him.

Rich would say, "nope I'm Rich. I'm your son-in-law. I'm married to Sandy."

"Boy you sure look like my dad."

Rich would say, "no I'm not."

Mistaken identity. it can be a compliment or not, and it's not meant to be either. It's just is who they think you are when they look at you. Try not to take offense, obviously sometimes it's hard not to do so, other times you're flattered. My dad thought I was my mom and I said to him, "What is your wife's name?"(I felt comfortable asking him this question because he had just called her by name.) He said "Loretta" I said, "What's my name? "He replied, "You're Sandy" I said, "That's right, so if I'm Sandy, I can't be Loretta. I'm your daughter." He looked at me all confused and I said, "I'm Tootles. You used to call me that. Now you call me San-dandy." He shook his head, started to smile and said, "Well, I'll be damned."

Let's Go Walk the Stores

Zzzzzz! The sound coming from the chair in the living room. Mom's biggest challenge, how to keep Dad involved, so he doesn't sit and sleep the day away. She had gotten pretty creative, but there were times when she was too tired to work with him or she just needed a break.

It was at those times that she would put Dad in the car and take him to the store. They would walk the aisles of whatever store Mom picked out. Taking their time looking at things, just taking up time, keeping busy, getting exercise and keeping him awake. She knew if he slept all day she would be up with him all night. They would, often times, take Tootsie with them as well. Dad would push the cart or carry Toots through the stores. It really was quite an endearing site.

We applauded Mom for doing this with Dad. If he was up, she would also walk the mall with him early in the mornings. Anything to keep him moving, exercising and awake. It didn't hurt that Mom got some exercise too.

We went on the belief that we needed to keep his body as well as his mind as active as possible. Yes, we did the crosswords and word finds, he also played solitaire until he no longer able to do that. But he could always walk and help with things, and that was a special blessing.

DVR Time

Television can be good and bad for those with Alzheimer's and dementia. First and foremost, just like we tell all new parents as well, it is not a babysitter! You cannot plunk a person down, switch on the 'tube' and expect them to stay content. However, there are times that you can find something that will really capture that particular persons interest and you might get to use the bathroom without worry. Of course, you still have to leave the bathroom door ajar so you can hear what is happening in the other room. We found that my dad really liked Jag, a naval series that was on. He also loved westerns and a lot of old time shows. Mom would put the reruns on during the day for him, and all would be fine until he had to use the bathroom.

He would come back and be all upset because he would know he missed some of the show. There wasn't much Mom could do, but explain to him that she was sorry, but that is just the way things were. Along comes the DVR! Yes! Exactly what she needed. She could hit the pause button. Take care of Dad and he could come back and take up where he had left off by Mom pushing play. Wonderful, he was happy. Mom was happy. All was well with the world.

If it was a tape that Mom had in the VCR or DVD she would be able to stop it and there would never be a problem. But it was when the show was on a TV station that this problem would occur so the DVR was just an amazing wonderful tool for her to be able to utilize.

The nice thing about having VCR and DVD players is that you can find old westerns, cartoons and variety shows that they used to watch when they were young, often times we could put one of those on when it was a bad day. It would settle him down to the point where he wouldn't remember what was upsetting him. My mom would resort to this as a last ditch effort, she always tried to do other things first to get his mind off of things. She never really did like putting him in front of the TV.

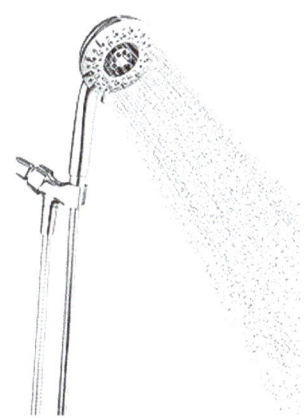

What is it About a Shower

If you go into nursing facility and hear screaming like someone is getting assaulted, it's a good bet you could've walked in on shower day. My grandmother hated to take a shower. And as my father progressed, he followed suit. Now with my grandmother, the aids at the nursing facility, gave the showers. And according to every account we heard it was no easy task. Senior citizens may look frail, but don't let that fool you, they can be strong as an ox if the situation calls for it. Shower day is the perfect situation.

For my dad, it didn't matter if you threatened or yelled he just wasn't going to do it. So for us the best way was to use finesse. "Do you want to go out and go for an ice cream? Sure, I'll take you, just as soon as you get your shower. Why? Because you are starting to stink and you'll make your ice cream melt." Whatever worked we did it to get him to shower.

I asked a friend who was a nurse in a facility with residents similar to my grandma and dad and she had some good reasons as to why you get this reaction on shower day.

1. Sometimes in facilities, the shower rooms can be daunting and the water temperature in the showers maybe cold.

2. To the patients they have to take off all their clothes in front of someone they don't know. Modesty, even at that age is important to recognize.

3. All of that can be very intimidating for someone who isn't suffering from memory loss. Put yourself in their place. You can see why they feel accosted.

4. For at home care, even if it's a loved one helping out. Taking a shower just isn't in their list of priorities anymore. They tend to lose their sense of smell, so they don't think they stink, they can't smell themselves.

Please, please don't force! You could end up injuring them or injuring yourself or both, try to figure a way around it. Try to figure ways to get them in, if it's too much wait until the next day, maybe it'll be a better day.

He Got Out of The Car!

It's 9 in the morning and my phone rings. I look at it and I see it's my mom and she's calling from her cell phone. I answered it and I hear her voice in a frantic but calm demeanor, say, "Sandy I'm on my way to the doctor. I can't turn around and your dad got out of the car on me at the corner. He's walking down the road back towards the condos. I need your help!" She went on to explain that she was headed in the direction of her doctor appointment and they were stopped at the traffic light when he got the door open and got out of the car. Of course, the light changed as he did this and she couldn't get him back in the car. She was in the left-hand turn lane and had to go. She saw that he was safely on the sidewalk and was headed in the right direction, but on the opposite side of the street, from where they lived. At the time there wasn't a place she could stop and turn around.

As she was explaining this to me, I was running around the house, getting my keys and my coat and jumping in the car. I headed towards where they lived. When I turned on the street where they lived off of, I became hyper vigilant looking for him on both sides of the street. Praying that I wouldn't see any police cars or ambulances because he got hit trying to cross a four lane street. On a whim I turned into the neighborhood opposite of where they lived, and I saw him walking along the sidewalk there. 'Thank You, God!' I pulled up next to him and stopped and called out to him, "Hey Dad! What are you doing?" He told me he was just out for a walk. So I asked if he was tired of walking and would he like me to take him home. He thought about it and he said he thought that was a great idea and he climbed in the car with me. If he wasn't ready to get in, I would have parked the car, got out and walked with him until he was tired.

Once I got him settled in the car and strapped in, said a quick prayer of thanksgiving, I quickly called Mom and told her I had him and all was well. We would be waiting for her to go to lunch when she got finished with her doctor's appointment.

This is a scenario many who have loved ones with this disease dread happening. This was before they had cars where the driver could lock the doors and windows. There were child locks on the doors in back, but Dad always rode upfront with mom as her navigator. We were blessed, Dad was safe, I was home. If I hadn't been home, she would've called 911 and turned around as soon as possible to get back to him.

Thankfully, today's vehicles have door and window locks, both were needed with Dad on several occasions. Mom invested in a new vehicle that had both of these safety features which she used without fail. If Dad had a tissue in his hand, he would try and open the window and throw it out. Any kind of garbage he had in his hand, he would try and throw it out the window so the window locks were definitely needed. Several other times he got confused and thought it was time to get out of the car when we were just stopped at a light. If we hadn't had the door locks on…who knows, but we did and so there were no worries.

Old Time Cartoons

Who remembers the old Looney Tunes cartoons? There was Fog Horn Leg Horn, Popeye, Tom and Jerry, Elmer Fud and Bugs Bunny, The Road Runner and Coyote. We also had Mr. Magoo, Rockey and Bullwinkle and Disney cartoons. Mickey Mouse, Donald Duck, Goofy the list goes on. These are the cartoons that my dad remembered so these are the cartoons that we looked for on VCR or DVDs. We also were able to find the shows that he listened to on radio like *The Shadow*. He enjoyed sitting and watching or listening to these when he was resting.

When the boys came over, they enjoyed watching them with him and if truth be told, I sat down and watched them with him sometimes as well. It was a great way to spend time with Dad, and we laughed at some of the silliness of the cartoons still today. It gave the boys a good look at what their Paps and parents grew up with on the black-and-white TV, and to listen to things on the radio and to see that things don't have to be in color and fast paced to be fun and to be enjoyed.

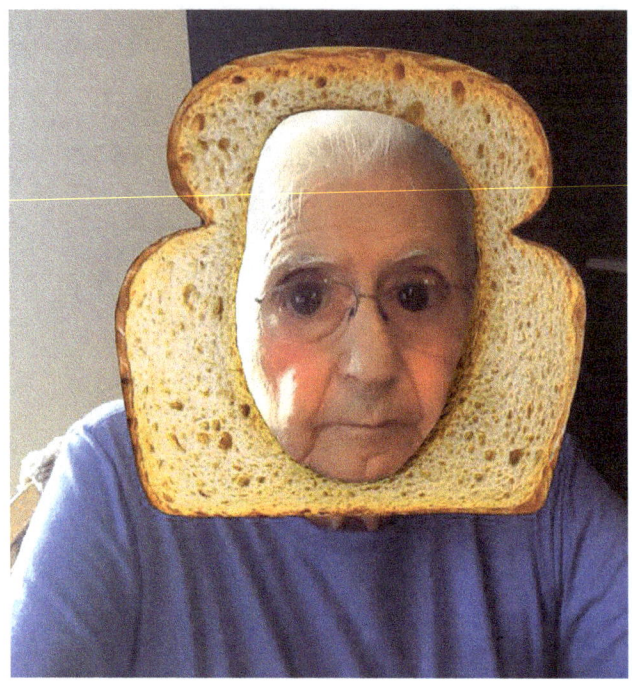

How the Hell Did He do That?

Working in the hospital I thought I had seen it all. Older people will just simply amaze you with how limber they can be, and how they can manage to get out of the restraints, which are put in place for their safety, in spite of your best efforts. Want to know more? Ask any medical professional that has worked in patient care either in a hospital, rehab, or nursing facility, there are plenty of OMG! Stories. But, of course, my dad has one.

At their home after Mom got Tootsie for my dad, she started leaving an old pair of Dad's slippers by the front door. This way she could quickly slip them on and get Toots out to do her duty, in the early morning or late evening if she happen to be barefooted.

One morning, she went to the front door to let the dog out, and was about to put her feet into the slippers, but something just didn't look quite right. Thankfully, she turned another light on, and sure enough, something was very very wrong! There was poop in the slippers. How did that happen? It couldn't have been Tootsie, she was in her crate all night. Besides, on further inspection, that could not have come out of Tootsie! "Oh, my word! How the hell did he do that?"

She stood there, looking at the slipper thinking to herself, "He had to have done it during the night. I can't believe I didn't wake up and hear him when he got up and wandered around. How did he manage THAT and not fall and hurt himself?"

His grandson, Ben, and many of us wonder to this day, the precision it took to get it all in the slippers and not on the floor! Especially when half the time he missed the toilet and he would be sitting down on that! We told Mom that she needs to put his slippers in the toilet that way she will never have to clean up a mess in the bathroom again. Problem solved!

Sometimes, you just have to laugh!

Who Lives Here?

When I got married, it was very important to me to have my grandmother at my wedding. I didn't care if she knew me or not I knew she would just love being there! The game plan was for the nursing home to get her hair done and have her showered. The limo would come to my house pick me, the bridesmaids, the junior bridesmaid and flower girls up and take us to the church to dress and get ready. My dad would then go with the limo to pick up Grandma. They would then bring her to the church and we would dress her there.

It all went according to plan. They even had a sendoff for Grandma, telling her they wanted to hear all about the wedding when she returned that evening. My dad escorted her out to the limo and coached her to get in letting her know he was right there with her. She got in, but then she asked him, "Who lives here? This is a beautiful home!"

I always felt it was so important to have my grandmother with us on all the family occasions. After the wedding, we had all the pictures taken with my mom and dad and grandma in them first. That way, Mom and Dad could take Grandma back and then get to the reception in time.

I look back, lovingly on these pictures 30 years later and I'm still satisfied that I made the decision that was right for me and Grandma. We worked out a plan that we knew wouldn't stress her. No, she didn't remember that she had been to a wedding when she returned to the nursing home. That was OK. We all knew that what Grandma would say, "It was wonderful! Wonderful!" And at the time that it was happening, she was thrilled to be there! You could tell that by the smile on her face!

IHOP Friends

Yes, Mom had her go to restaurants to take Dad to, but there was one that was their absolute favorite. It was IHOP off of Fields Ertel Road. There we met, Eulie, Lamont, Jessica, Sam and Anthony, to name a few. Whenever Dad was at his worst, she knew she could go in there and sit there with dad and they would bring coffee and pancakes or whatever muffin they had and if it wasn't busy, they would sit there and they would talk with mom and dad. They truly cared about mom and dad. If Rich and I came for lunch on a day that my parents had been there, they were quick to come over and tell us that Dad was having a bad day and we needed to go check on them. Often times they would give Mom and Dad their food for free just because. The crew was always there with a smile. Took the time to give and share, and to just be friends.

On the day that my dad passed. Our immediate family all went to IHOP for breakfast and they knew right away because Dad wasn't with us. They were so sad, Sam ran over to the store across the way, she bought flowers and a card and they all signed that card and came to the table, brought the flowers to Mom and said how much they were going to miss Dad. They gave us all hugs, but Mom got extra special long bear hugs. We took them a copy of the obituary and told them please if they could to come to the visitation and the burial because they had become like family to us.

We continued to go to the IHOP until it closed unfortunately. Lamont and Jessica and Sam were always quick to get us seated, especially if Mom came by herself. They just treated her like gold and it was just so nice to know that she was taken care of any time that she walked through those doors. I often wonder if the people at the IHOP main office knew just what a special group of people they had. My brother said he was going to write in and tell them. I hoped they would have done something special for them. But even if they didn't get anything special, they knew they had a special place in our hearts that will never ever go away, or will be forgotten. As Lamont would say, "We got you!"

Chickens in the Freezer

There was an evening that my dad was not feeling well. When this happened it often caused him more confusion. I was at my parents' home on this particular evening, and he was really unsettled. He kept going to bed because he was cold, but then he would come back out to the living room again. On one particular trip, he stopped and asked if the chickens were in the freezer. I looked at Mom. She shrugged her shoulders in a 'I don't know' sign so I just answered him that they were.

This happened a couple more times. We kept assuring him that the chickens were in the freezer and trying to get his mind on something else. In between questions, we were trying to figure out what was on his mind that he kept asking the same question over again.

Finally, I remembered that he worked in engine test for jet engines and in order to simulate bird strikes in the air, they would throw frozen chickens in the cell during the test and check for damage. So I asked him if he was asking about the chickens for the engine test. He looked at me like I had two heads and said, "Well, yeah. What the hell did you think I meant?" I just told him I was checking to make sure that they were needed. He proceeded to rattled off how many pounds and in which test cell they were needed. I assured him we had enough and they would be ready to go. He turned around went back to bed, covered up and went to sleep.

Mom and I were both glad that I remembered what my dad did when he was employed and even happier that he often talked about what they did when they would test the engines. How they would break everything down, clean it and put it back together again and run additional testing.

Try try try to know the backstory of the person who has Alzheimer's and dementia. It can save you and that person a lot of frustration. This story in particular shows if we had not known Dad's backstory and work history, his whole night would have been nothing but frustration. He would have been getting up and down probably most of the night wondering about those frozen chickens. Mom would've been worried that he was getting sicker and that's why he was getting up and down and that he wasn't getting enough rest. What in the world made him think of those chickens? We don't know. Maybe he heard a jet flyover, who knows. It came out of the blue that's for sure. I had an angel sitting on my shoulder, whispering in my ear, telling me what it was all about. I don't know how it came into my mind what it was, but I'm sure glad it did.

Just Like Riding a Bike

My dad landed in Germany on his 18th birthday. He was in the Air Force and his assignment was in Birkenfeld, Germany. He was assigned to the 602 AC&W Squadron, Der Vogelhund or the bird dog and their call signal was Cornbeef Control. This unit would guide the airplanes for the Berlin airlift. One of the war's, many unsung heroes. He sat up in the radio tower sending and receiving Morse code often keeping the planes on track if they were fogged in and sending the coordinates in order for them to either reach their destination or return home. This was his life for a little more than 3 years.

In August of 2015, the retired World War II USS LST 325 naval ship sailed down the Ohio River making a stop in Cincinnati. My Uncle Bill took my dad, my mom and our youngest son, Nathan, downtown to do a tour of this retired war ship that came into town. This ship was very similar to the one Dad had crossed the ocean on. That ship was the USS T. Henry Gibbins. When they were on the retired ship, Dad was pointing out different things about the radio. It was funny because most of the people on that ship had no idea what most of those dials and switches were for. Dad explained what he did, along with my uncle and my mom's help, when he was in the Air Force. They allowed him to cross over the lines that kept the tourist out and sit down at the radio desk. Dad showed them all how everything worked and what each thing was for. They were impressed with his memory and recall.

Although the radio was dead, and not hooked up to anything. Dad was so transfixed and back in time that he actually thought he could hear radio signals coming across the headset and was working on decoding them in order to help the pilots out. That is how vivid the memory was when he sat down with those headsets on and in front of that radio once again. I really wish that they would have been able to have made a video of it. I would've loved to have seen that as I'm sure the rest of the family would have too. But as with all things, Alzheimer's, you just never know when something is going to happen. especially something that special.

Dad Loved his Beer

Aaawwww! That wonderful refreshing taste of a nice cold beer on a hot summer day. For my dad it didn't matter what the weather was, a good cold beer was a nice cold beer. Growing up my dad always gave us little glasses of beer that we would drink along with him. He had to switch to quarts of beer because by the time he was finished giving us little drinks, and my mom got her drink his bottle would be empty.

When I came home from college, my brother had finished the basement in my parents' home after they had to replace the furnace, and a beer tap was installed. It held a pony keg of Little Kings Cream Ale. Well, of course, all of the New Year's Eve parties were held in our house. Then came the news from the doctor, Dad had to give up his beer because his blood pressure was getting too high. He did this just like that! One day he had a drink of beer the next day he didn't. Shortly there after the company that made Little Kings shut down their third shift. We all laughed and said it was because Dad quit drinking it.

When they came out with non-alcoholic beer, we were thrilled. O'Doul's Amber quickly became his favorite. He would have two bottles a day. But even then the doctor warned us that we shouldn't give him too much because it still had a very small amount of alcohol percentage in it. What we didn't know was that non-alcoholic beer can have an alcohol beverage volume of up to 0.5% and still be labeled non-alcoholic, legally. O'Doul's has around 0.4%.

Later years, he was starting to want it in the morning so Mom would save a bottle and put tea or apple juice in the bottle and she would just set it by him and he would taste it and he say, "This doesn't taste right." Mom would say, "It's beer, drink it, it's cold." Sometimes he would drink it sometimes he wouldn't. But just having the bottle sitting there next to him seemed to be OK. It couldn't be empty, though it had to have something in it, and not water.

Tom is Fishing For Dad

It was Father's Day, and my brother and his wife took my mom and dad out to their beautiful place in Indiana, we all call it a slice of heaven, to spend the day fishing. Tom set Dad up on the edge of the one pond and told Dad to just stay seated there and fish from the chair. My mom remembers having a discussion with Tom about how she didn't think that location would work. Evidently, there was a slight slope and at that time, Dad was having some issues with balance. My brother assured her it would be just fine.

They proceeded on with their day and my mom settled in for a relaxing afternoon. Well, it didn't take long before Dad got a bite. He always got up when he got a bite, so what did he do? He got up out of his chair to try and set the hook and land the fish. Tom, of course, cautioned Dad to keep seated, and he would make sure he got the fish as Dad brought them in. Several more times of the up-and-down scenario and the inevitable happened. Dad gets a bite, gets up and WHOOPS! In the pond he goes! Tom had to go in after him and help him out and then go back in to find Dad's glasses. Mom, meanwhile, has been sitting in her chair on the shoreline, laughing like crazy.

In hindsight, I think Tom wishes he may have put more stock into what Mom was saying. But even if she hadn't been there, Tom would never have knowingly set Dad up in a situation that could have caused him harm. My Dad loved to swim so he most probably enjoyed the dip in the water.

Tom also is in the medical field, and he would never have put himself or my dad in a situation where he couldn't render aid. There was always two people there whenever they were at their place in the country. Should there have been an emergency he would've been able to render immediate assistance, while someone else could call for additional assistance if needed. But I do think that Dad was the biggest fish Tom ever caught.

Friendly's

Ice cream! Ice cream! We all scream for ice cream! There was this great ice cream parlor restaurant, not far from where my grandmother lived in her nursing facility. My sister and I always enjoyed going and taking her out for lunch and an ice cream. One of us always had to go in first and clear off the table of all the condiments or else they would find their way into Grandmas' pockets.

We would order her food, she liked burgers and french fries. She always complained that she just couldn't eat all that food. Our response was always the same, "Just eat what you want." She would always eat it all except for the tips of the french fries. For some reason, she always broke those off and ate the rest of the fry. Then, of course, she had to have an ice cream sundae for dessert. She wasn't happy when it was served to her and she saw the size of it. Why she couldn't possibly eat it all, it was just too large. But somehow the spoon always found the bottom of that dish.

Deb and I always enjoyed taking Grandma out as much as she enjoyed being out. No, she didn't always know who we were, especially in her later years. She very seldom knew us, but it was fun and a special time for us.

One thing to note is that a lot of Alzheimer's and dementia patients don't remember the last time they ate. Sometimes they think they haven't eaten at all when they have just eaten five minutes ago and they will sit there and eat another full meal!

Not always do people with Alzheimer's enjoy going out, and sometimes they do. It just depends on the day and how the subject is approached. If you are turned down, the next time you wish to take them out, try a different approach. Maybe it was your approach that put them off. Were you in a hurry? Were you pushy? Were you demanding? All of these things will have them digging their heels in. So if one time you get a negative answer, don't give up trying. You will be robbing both of you of some pleasant and wonderful times spent together. If they don't want to go out, stay there with them and spend some quality time with them there. It doesn't really matter if they remember who you are. Don't quiz them about it, just tell them who you are and what you would like to do and where you want to go. If they say, "that's stupid" which we got quite often, that's OK. Have fun with it and bring them around to it without forcing it. For something being so "stupid" Grandma sure ate a lot of ice cream Sundaes.

Weren't You in the Marching Band?

Gary, my cousin and his family always stayed with my parents whenever they came into town from Atlanta, Georgia. In fact, they still do. We always have fun, especially at Christmas time. We usually go to the Krohn's Conservatory to see the stunning Christmas display. And of course, we always have to hit all the local restaurants like Skyline, LaRosa's, Perkins, you name it we hit them all especially United Dairy Farmers for the malts. Gary's dad, Bill, would join us and sometimes his brother David and his family. My sister and brother and their families would come and we made it a family affair.

One year, my dad asked Gary if he was the drum major of the Roger Bacon high school band and didn't they go to school together? Gary explain that no, it wasn't him. His usual answer was he didn't attend Roger Bacon high school, and that Gary was his nephew. But for some reason, Dad just couldn't let this go. Throughout their stay, he kept circling back to it and asking him if he was the drum major for Roger Bacon's band. My mom finally stepped in and pointed out the age difference between the two of them and it stopped.

Until the next time they came to visit. This went on for about two years or so. Finally, my exasperated mom, said, "For crying out loud! Can't you see you are way older, and he wasn't even close to being born when you were in high school?" Now that seem to do the trick.

My guess is Gary just resembled that young man that was the drum major when my father attended Roger Bacon high school. Dad just could not get it out of his mind. My dad always was good at mathematics, could always do very complicated problems in his head without using pencil and paper, so maybe when Mom asked him to consider this problem, some part of his brain was able to work that out and it computed. Whatever the reason it worked and the questioning stopped. The good thing about this is that Gary was so patient with Dad and very understanding. It just made things so much easier knowing that people understood, were not judgmental and loved him as he was.

Alarm and Padlocks

"I've got to get some sleep" Mom lamented. She needed to find a way that she could sleep soundly and not have to worry about Dad wandering around and getting out of the house at night. Often, as is the case with people with Alzheimer's and dementia, they do wander at night. So my youngest, Nate, helped my mom find door alarms that go off and make the most obnoxious buzz in order to wake Mom up, or to alert her if it happened during the day and he was out of her line of sight.

This worked really well, but even with this, the escape artist would find a way to get out. So... Along with the alarms, Mom found a really small padlock, luggage padlocks with tiny keys. Just enough to keep him in, but not enough to keep emergency response from getting in if needed. This, too, worked for a while, until he found where Mom kept the keys. They were always near the locks and he would open them up and go outside and or lose the key. Usually this wasn't a problem, Mom could get him to come back in and often times they went for some not so romantic moonlight walks in their pajamas. Mom finally found hiding places for the keys that he was unable to discover, and was able to keep the keys there.

First off, buy extra locks that take the same key, like I said, they do go missing on occasion. Second, please don't judge us for this. It worked for us and it beats the alternative of having him wander off and get lost and or hurt. It was an instrument that would buy us the extra time to get to him and get his attention directed on to something else.

Keep in mind. As I said, in the prologue, this is not a "how to" manual. It is stories of my family, and what we did. Enjoy them, use some, whatever. It is not the final say or only word in the situation by any means. Find the answer that is safe for you and your circumstance. This is what will work for your family.

SANDY TOMLIN

Have You Seen my Dog?

Despite having alarms and locks on the doors, my dad still gave my mom the slip on two different occasions. The first time was at 11 PM, thankfully on a warm summer night. Mom still doesn't know how he managed to get past her and she didn't hear the door alarms go off. When she realized that he wasn't in the bathroom, she took off running outside. She looked up and down the street-no sign of him. All she could think was, 'please God don't let him have headed for the lake' that was behind where they lived. Or that he was headed to the busy street at the entrance of their subdivision.

She tamped down her panic and dialed 911 and explain the situation to them and my father's health issues. They were quickly on their way. Mom called me next, and I jumped in my car and headed over to their home. My brother and I only live about 5 miles away, so I got there pretty quickly as well. As I entered the community where they live, I saw the police car at the opposite end of the street from where they live. Unfortunately, it was also very close to the busy four lane road. I drove up and walked up to the police officer, and explain who I was. He quickly pointed me in the direction of where my dad was. I called my mom and told her we had him and would be home soon.

He had climbed the separating fence and had fallen on some rocks. He was sitting down explaining to the officers that he had lost his dog. I came up, and thankfully he knew me, and said, "San-dandy!" I greeted him and asked what he was doing. He said he was looking for Spitzy. That was his boyhood dog. I said, "Dad, Spitz beat you home! Come on I'll take you there." He got up with the help of the police department. Who had smiles on their faces. By that time Mom was there giving hugs and apologizing. We took him to the ER where they checked him over, and he had a bruised knee and some scrapes.

We were very lucky this had a good outcome! The police were quick, efficient, and great with Dad! I was lucky I knew Spitzy was the name of his dog when he was a boy and that he recognized me that day. Moral of the story. Have a plan in place. Even if you think they can't get out they can. Don't wait to call 911. It makes a difference!

Who's the Cute Fat Baby?

January 30, 1998, my cousin Gary's first born came into this world. He was the first grandchild for my Uncle Bill. Sadly, my Aunt Kathy passed a little more than a year before. They had come up for his brother, David's wedding, and while they were in town, they took advantage and came to visit Grandma and get a four generation picture with her.

When they went to introduce Alexander to Grandma and put him in her lap, she was thrilled. She turned to them and asked, "Who does this cute little fat baby belong to?" They all had a good chuckle, and explained again that this was her great grandson. In fact, it was her fifth great grandchild.

I am not sure if she was happier because she was holding this cute little fat baby or because it was her great grandson. We'll call it a tie.

Going into the nursing home to see Grandma, Gary and Gloria's expectations weren't high. So when there was no recognition, there was no sadness. They didn't set themselves up for that, and therefore, their moods weren't deflated, but remained joyous, and happy.

Grandma was really enjoying herself, regardless, if she knew who it was and they were thrilled that they could see her being so happy. Life doesn't get much better than that!

Pee with the Ladies

Incontinence for Alzheimer's and dementia patients, it's just a fact of life. It's a normal progression of the disease. Mom always carried extra sets of clothing, and the Depends underware in the car for Dad. It wasn't always convenient to find a place to change him. There were no family washrooms at the time, just men's and women's restrooms. If she could, she would get him changed in the car, but overtime even that became difficult. She had no choice except to take him into the ladies room with her. Sometimes she would luck out and it would be what we called, 'a single holer'. But more often than not, she would have to go into a multi use restroom for women. If I had him out being my bag man, there were times when I had to take him into the ladies room with me too.

Dad would be so funny, he would say that he gets to pee with the ladies and how lucky he was. Mom would just walk in with him in tow. Explain the situation and take him into a stall and do what she needed to do to take care of him. The nice thing is that women usually are so understanding and accommodating. I can't remember a time hearing my mom mentioning anyone objecting to my father coming in to "Pee with the ladies" it always felt like he was immediately welcomed with no hostility, at least the times that I took him in or was with Mom when she took him in, that is how it felt.

No matter how hard things were, we were always better when Dad was with us. People were more patient and understanding, accommodating and helpful, quite frankly the world anyone would want to live in, and the way we all should treat one another. Why does it take a child or an elderly person with an infirmity to bring out the best in humanity?

I was taught there is a reason for everything. Maybe Alzheimer's and dementia is how we are supposed to learn compassion, patience, and the deepest caring love possible. The kind that makes you cry at the happiness to be able to partake in such an opportunity, be thankful for it and learn from it. To learn what true love really is.

Music

Mitch Miller, John, Philip Sousa, Ray Conniff Singers, Spike Jones, Louis Armstrong, and Knuckles O'Toole. These were just a few of my dad's favorite artist. Growing up, we would watch the different variety shows such as Lawrence Welk, Dean Martin and Frank Sinatra and of course Ed Sullivan. We listen to albums all the time.

One way of keeping Dad calm was to play his favorite songs and music. He would be singing and humming along to the melodies and he would know the words. Often times he made up versus that always made us laugh. Once, while my niece, Jennifer was sitting with my father, while my mother had a test done at the hospital, the comics weren't working. Since they were at mom and dad's house, she resorted to putting on music that he liked. It worked like a charm.

My oldest son, Ben, was in the high school chorus. The new choir Director that took over in his sophomore year was just really great. Mom and I did all the fitting and alterations for all the different choirs. The sizing had to be done while school was in session, so Dad always came along with us. He would sit in the back of the class and sing or enjoy the music while Mom and I worked with the students. Of course, he always had Tootsie with him as well.

After the first year, Jason, the choir Director came to me and asked what type of music my dad enjoyed. That year he made a special point of including music for each choir to sing, that they all knew they were singing, especially for him. That was one concert he thoroughly enjoyed. He sat there he clapped, he sang, his toe tapped. It was wonderful to see how those kids touched his heart and made his evening. Just a wonderful experience for him. I was in school the next day and I went to every class and made sure I thanked them personally for what they had done for my dad and told them just how much it meant to my dad and how much it meant to my family that they provided such a beautiful service.

My nieces, who also attended the same high school, years before, were in the marching and symphony bands. On one occasion, the symphony band was given the honor to premier the piece called "October" by Eric Whitaker. My niece, Christi, did a personal dedication to her grandfather as she played that piece. We could see her emotions as she played. To us, the band never sounded so beautiful, nor will it ever again!

Music, soothes the savage beast, isn't too far from wrong. Lots of research has been done on the benefits of music for certain diseases. Parkinson's disease is another one where music is very advantageous. Children's Hospital has an entire music therapy department that helps the children especially those that are there longer than a few days, cope with what is going on with them. It's a wonderful thing to incorporate into caring for your loved ones with Alzheimer's and dementia.

Stevie Baby!

Our primary care physician was one in a million! His name was Stephen Berg. My sister and I both worked with him when he was going through his residency. You could already see he was going to be one of the good ones.

When my grandmother was first diagnosed, we were referred by her neurologist, to a doctor, who was just starting his practice as an internist, and who specialized in geriatric care. When he said Dr. Stephen Berg, I was thrilled! It wasn't long before the entire family was under his care. We were like family. Never could you leave the office without a joke and a smile and of course, one of his big bear hugs. He was a physician who truly cared for his patients and took the time to talk and listen to them.

My dad would walk into the office and catch sight of him and say in a booming voice, "Stevie baby! How the hell are you?" Dr. Berg would always stop and greet him. If you were in a patient's room, waiting to be seen, you could hear the two of them laughing and carrying on through the walls. Dr. Berg assembled a great team around him as well: Gina, Mary Ann, Kristen, Jen, and of course, Karen, who was always there and Becky his nurse practitioner. When my grandmother, and then again, when my father died, Steve called and spoke to us personally. How often does that happen these days?

Dr. Stephen Berg died while working at his desk in his office doing what he loved. It came as a shock to all of us because we still considered him a young man. He was irreplaceable, and it took us some time to find another practice to call home. We were fortunate enough to find out what office Becky went to, and we followed her.

She is doing an amazing job, carrying the torch and caring for us the way "Stevie baby" did. And we laugh and tell jokes, and wonder what in the world the good Lord was thinking when he called both of them home. I bet they never stop laughing in heaven.

Hup 2, 3, 4

Oh, no! Dad is in the hospital. Dad had some other medical issues that caused the need for him to be sedated. The problem was, he didn't want to wake up for two days after they gave it to him. Once he did wake up, he was extremely weak and just had no strength.

Because of this Dad had to go to physical therapy to help get his strength back and get him moving again. One of the exercises was to get him to lift his feet up and down while standing up and then to walk. They couldn't get him to understand what he needed to do. Knowing that Dad loved the military drill and the color guard, I started calling out cadence, "Hup 2, 3, 4" the shoulders squared, the feet came up and off we went. The physical therapist was thrilled with this turn of events. When he was transferred to the rehab hospital. The trick was passed along in the notes and report and he was able to graduate in record time.

Stays in the hospital takes the entire family to pitch in. Everyone takes a shift to stay and help out. Mom usually took the night shift because that tended to be his bad time. One night my then 15-year-old son told his Nana to go home and go to bed. He was going to stay the night with his Paps and take care of him. Nana told him, "He has accidents at night. You'll have to call the nurses to let them know that he has had an accident." Ben said, "Don't worry Nana, I'll take care of it." As luck would have it, Dad had an accident in the middle of the night. Ben called out to the nurses station to let them know that he had an accident. However, they were so used to Mom taking care of it, that they just brought in the clean pad and sheets and left them there. So Ben took care of it. He cleaned his Paps up and gave him a clean bed to boot. Not all families are this lucky, but we sure are!

Sonny's Angels

After my dad passed, the trucking company that his great niece worked for was a huge sponsor for the Alzheimer's walk. Jennifer became very involved with the event and helped organize it.

She also started a team named "Sonny's Angels": my dad's nickname. Every year, those who can make it head out to Batesville, Indiana, and walk for the cure for Alzheimer's disease.

What a wonderful tribute to my dad, and it really touched our family that she cared so much for her Uncle Sonny that she would do this.

There are walks for Alzheimer's all over the country if you go to www.alz.org you will be able to find the nearest one to you. It's very worthwhile and rewarding. Each dollar raised gets us closer to finding a cure for this disease. Save the memories! They are precious!

Get involved! www.ALZ.org

"...in Ohio, more than 236,200 people are living with Alzheimer's. 452,000 caregivers dedicate 679 million hours of unpaid care. From southern Ohio to southern Indiana to Northern Kentucky and every town in between" there is an Alzheimer's chapter that can help.

"Whether offering support to someone facing Alzheimer's, advocating for the needs and rights of those facing Dementia, Or advancing critical research, we work towards methods of treatment, prevention, and ultimately a cure." alz.org

Greater Cincinnati Chapter
Sawyer Point Building
720 E. Pete Rose Way Suite 330
Cincinnati, Ohio. 45202
513.721.4284

EVENTS Community Resource Finder, 24/7 hotline, 800.272.3900

Mother' Day

My grandmother lived to be 91 years old. She was just a beautiful soul both inside and out. She loved her Sonny boy (my dad) and Billy (his younger brother of eight years). She was an awesome grandmother, as well.

When she became ill, to the point where we knew this was probably going to be her time, my dad never left her side. The last day or so she wasn't communicative, Dad talked to her almost nonstop. Around 10 PM in the evening Dad, who now had the diagnosis of Alzheimer's and Dementia, somehow figured out that the next day was Mother's Day. Maybe he heard the nurses talking, we aren't sure, but he asked his mom for one more favor, "Mom, I know you are wanting to go home, but if you would hold on just a few hours for me and leave on Mother's Day. I sure would appreciate it."

She must've heard him because around 3 AM, as my mom was helping a nurse clean her up, they rolled her over and Mom could feel her body relax. She granted her Sonny boy one last wish.

May 14, 2000. My grandmother's last Mother's Day, and my first Mother's Day. It was a day of celebration all the way around. A day to celebrate a beautiful life and mother. A day to celebrate all mothers that have blessed us. And a day, as I will always remember as the day my grandma passed the torch to me. Her last Mother's Day, and my first! Thanks, Grandma!

Cracker Jack Ring

Cracker Jacks. Who doesn't love them? And the prize inside, finding it is always so much fun. One day, Mom and Dad were splitting a box of Cracker Jacks. As they made their way through the box, Dad found the prize. It was a ring. He turned to Mom and proposed to her with the Cracker Jack prize ring.

He didn't realize it, but he already had the prize for more than 60 years. What he did realize was the love he felt for her. That light never dimmed.

I don't know what else I can add except that Love is a wonderful thing!

Well done, Thou good and faithful servant....

George C. Wolf, Jr.
March 13, 1931 to July 27, 2018

Epilogue

On the evening of July 27, 2018, my mom called and said that she was taking Dad to the hospital because he had not been feeling good all day and had been throwing up. For some reason I just didn't want her to drive him to the hospital if he was sick so I told her to wait and I'd come over and drive them to the hospital. When I got there, Mom was getting Dad up and getting ready to walk him to the car. I took one arm she took the other, and we got out as far as the hallway and Dad had to sit down. I looked at his nail beds, and I said, "Mom, call 911 Dad needs some help". As I was talking to the 911 operator, Dad stopped breathing I said to him, "Dammit Dad don't you do this to me" but when I looked at him again, his face was beautiful, and I knew he was gone. I knew he was in heaven gazing at the face of God. I did CPR until the paramedics arrived. I told them that he was gone, but they couldn't stop until we could present his living will and Do not resuscitate papers. I quickly called Tom to come over, called my sister, sort of, my niece happened to have her phone. I felt so bad for my sister, she was in South Carolina and could do nothing. Not that we could do much more, but we were there with Mom and Dad. When they stopped we had to leave the house because it was a crime scene at that point and we had to wait for the coroner to come.

I walked outside with Mom and her neighbors were all there giving her support. After the coroner came Mom was allowed one more kiss and Tom assisted the coroner with Dad's body. I don't know how he did it, He said it was his honor to do it.

Dad's visitation was very well attended by friends and family. He was buried in his Air Force uniform and his coffin draped with an American flag. Mass of a Christian burial was held at our Parish and the choir sang the mass, with our dear family friend Beth singing the lead solo on many of the songs. As we processed out, the choir director played "Glory Glory Hallelujah!"

Dad's coffin was wrapped in the American flag and placed behind a WWII Jeep where he took his final ride to the cemetery. As we drove along, people were pulling over and stopping, some taking pictures, several saluting, many placing their hands over their hearts. We were so happy for Dad!

At the cemetery, after all the burial rights were finished, the American Legion Color guard preformed a ceremony. They folded the flag and presented it to Mom. A twenty one gun salute was made and the bugler sounded "Taps". Sadly, that was it for the places we would go with Dad here on this earth. I'm really going to miss the fun we had on our adventures together, but I look forward to more to come in the hereafter!

We all adjourned back to their home where the celebration of life continued.

To this day, it is hard to do or say something that doesn't remind us of Dad and it makes us smile or laugh right out loud. He has left a beautiful legacy of love, service and humor!

What a trip!

Thank You!

Thanks and all glory to God for the help and inspiration in writing this book.

Mom, thank you for your drive! If it weren't for your tenacious spirit, willingness and love to keep Dad at home; we, as a family, would never have been privileged to hear, see and know Dad's stories. We sure would have missed out on a most valuable gift. I love you, Mom. You are the best!

To my main cheerleader, friend, sister, family, Beth. You have been a constant source of encouragement from the beginning. Your time, suggestions and love have been invaluable. Without your spoken words, rallying me forward, I'm not sure I ever would have put pen to paper.

Don Tassone, my mentor. Your ideas, suggestions and help-just priceless! I will always be in debt to you for the time and talent you gave to this project and kindness that you bestowed upon me. What a gift!

To all my family and friends who encouraged me, submitted stories, pictures, even x-rays! You did this in order to help me make this book happen. I truly thank you all.

Cathy, Becky, Beth, Don and Rich- thank you for taking your time to read the manuscript. Through your words, suggestions and help, it has now become a competed project.

Rich, you are one in a billion! You listened tirelessly, gave thoughtful advice. You took over taking care of the house and everything that needed to be done, brought me drinks, dinner. No matter what I needed, you were there! I thank God every day for you. You were amazing with Dad and for that, I can't thank you enough. I love you, Babe!

References

1. "Helping kids also helps 82-year-old" by Michael D. Clark; The Cincinnati Enquirer. Rewrite permission given by Beryl Love, Editor & VP of News, The Enquirer Regional Editor, USA TODAY Network Ohio on July 9, 2025.

2. "Grandpa Remains Active in Class" by Tracey Carson. Rewrite permission given by Tracey Carson, Mason, Central Office on July 9; 2025.

3. *Good Night Gorilla* by Peggy Rathmann. Copyright held by and published by Peggy Rathmann 1994.

4. Cracker Jack. Owned by Frito Lay division of PepsiCo, Purchase New York. Registration #87058355 in 2016.

5. Charleston Chew. Owned by Tootsie Roll Industries, LLC, Chicago Illinois. Registration #928401 in 1971.

6. Little Kings Cream Ale, Hudepohl Brewing Company, Ohio

7. American Kennel Club. The AKC. https://www.akc.org

8. Honor Flight. http://honorflight.org or http://honorflighttri-state.org. Honor Flight Tri-State, 8627 Calumet Way, Cincinnati, OH 45249

9. Alzheimer's Association. Http://ALZ.org . Greater Cincinnati Chapter, Sawyer Point Building, 720 E. Pete Rose Way Suite 330, Cincinnati, OH 45202. 513.721.4284

10. O'Doul's Amber, Anheuser-Bush, Inc. 1200 Lynch St., St. Louis, MO 63118 www.anheuser-bush.com

11. ©Thomas Kincade Estate all rights reserved

www.ingramcontent.com/pod-product-compliance
Lightning Source LLC
LaVergne TN
LVHW081316060526
838201LV00005B/177